T0384273

The Political Economy of Financial Development in Malaysia

Current inquiries into the political economy of financial policymaking in Malaysia tend to focus on the high-level drama of crisis politics or simply point to the limited impact of post-crisis financial reforms, given that politico-business relations have remained close. In so doing, pundits ignore a number of intriguing questions: what is the relationship between financial development and financialisation and how has it played out in the Malaysian context? And more generally: how can a country like Malaysia become significantly more financially developed, yet fail to emancipate the financial system from political control; a core element of the financial development discourse?

To unravel the complexities of this puzzle, this book subjects the history and contemporary practices of financial policymaking in Malaysia to scrutiny. It argues that to understand financial development in Malaysia, its progress and reversals, it is important to conceptualise it as a political, rather than a merely technical process. In so doing, the book echoes a more profound concern in the political economy literature, namely the evolving relationship between states and markets, and the supposed retreat or reassertion of the state at a time of increasing (financial) globalisation. The book generates further insights into the evolving role of the state with regard to broader processes of development and marketisation, as they relate specifically to finance.

Lena Rethel is Associate Professor of International Political Economy at the University of Warwick.

Routledge Focus on Economics and Finance

The fields of economics are constantly expanding and evolving. This growth presents challenges for readers trying to keep up with the latest important insights. Routledge Focus on Economics and Finance presents short books on the latest big topics, linking in with the most cutting-edge economics research.

Individually, each title in the series provides coverage of a key academic topic, whilst collectively the series forms a comprehensive collection across the whole spectrum of economics.

Knowledge Infrastructure and Higher Education in India
Kaushalesh Lal and Shampa Paul

What Drives China's Economy
Economic, Socio-Political, Historical and Cultural Factors
Qing-Ping Ma

Environmentally Sustainable Industrial Development in China
Yanqing Jiang and Xu Yuan

The China–US Trade War
Guoyong Liang and Haoyuan Ding

Analyzing Electoral Promises with Game Theory
Yasushi Asako

The Political Economy of Financial Development in Malaysia
From the Asian Crisis to 1MDB
Lena Rethel

For more information about this series, please visit www.routledge.com/Routledge-Focus-on-Economics-and-Finance/book-series/RFEF

The Political Economy of Financial Development in Malaysia

From the Asian Crisis to 1MDB

Lena Rethel

Routledge
Taylor & Francis Group

LONDON AND NEW YORK

First published 2021
by Routledge
2 Park Square, Milton Park, Abingdon, Oxon OX14 4RN

and by Routledge
52 Vanderbilt Avenue, New York, NY 10017

Routledge is an imprint of the Taylor & Francis Group, an informa business

British Library Cataloguing in Publication Data
A catalogue record for this book is available from the British Library

Library of Congress Cataloging in Publication Data
A catalog record for this book has been requested

ISBN: 978-0-367-13869-1 (hbk)
ISBN: 978-0-429-02900-4 (ebk)

Typeset in Times New Roman
by Newgen Publishing UK

Contents

Figures

Tables

Preface

This book owes much to my Malaysian interlocutors and their uniquely positioned insights into the political economy and financial system of Malaysia during an unparalleled period of development, restructuring and transformation. I am sincerely thankful for the generosity with which they shared their views. When I visited Malaysia back in October 2018 to attend the biannual Global Islamic Finance Forum, organised under the theme of 'Value-Based Intermediation – Beyond Profit', I happened to pick up some books from local book shops which included recent exposés of the emerging 1MDB scandal. By their very nature, these books focused on the juicier bits of the scandal that has held Malaysians – and many observers abroad – in its grip and ultimately contributed to the historic victory of the opposition in the May 2018 election.

However, amongst the resulting discussion, I felt that the scandal drowned out the real progress Malaysia had made with reforming its financial system since the Asian crisis of the late 1990s. Yes, Malaysia was yet again in the grip of a financial scandal, but it had also come through the global financial crisis of 2008–2009 relatively unscathed. While not all of these reforms were uncontested and not all of them resulted unambiguously in the betterment of the socio-economic situation of the Malaysian people, they had nevertheless created a more resilient financial system, which made the 1MDB scandal stand out all the more.

In thinking through the arguments of this book, I benefited immensely from the paper presentations and discussions at the workshop 'How to Conceptualise Financialisation in Developing and Emerging Economies? Manifestations, Drivers and Implications', held at Girton College, University of Cambridge, in December 2018. I thank the organisers, Carolina Alves, Bruno Bonizzi and Annina Kaltenbrunner, for putting together such a spectacular event that firmly emplaced the topic of financialisation in emerging economies on the scholarly agenda.

There are also a number of people and institutions to whom I am grateful for their support during the writing process, once the initial idea for this book had taken shape. I thank the Oxford Centre for Islamic Studies and its Islamic Finance Research Unit for hosting me during my research leave. It was a great pleasure to interact with Islamic finance researchers from around the world, including many Malaysians, testament to the country's highly sophisticated Islamic finance sector.

My thanks also go to the University of Warwick for granting me the research time to write this book and specifically to my wonderful colleagues in the Department of Politics and International Studies. Juanita Elias deserves my special thanks for many stimulating conversations about the Malaysian political economy. I thank Ana Fraga for her research assistance and diligent compilation of Appendix A.

Furthermore, the three anonymous reviewers of the proposal offered some very necessary enthusiasm that convinced me to go ahead with this project and that I herewith gratefully acknowledge. I also thank Yongling Lam and Samantha Phua at Routledge for their encouragement. It is needless to say that all errors and interpretations are my own.

Last but not least, I thank Peter Cain for his enduring support of my work and providing companionship during my travels.

Abbreviations

1MDB	1Malaysia Development Berhad
ACMF	ASEAN Capital Markets Forum
ADB	Asian Development Bank
AFC	Asian financial crisis
ASEAN	Association of Southeast Asian Nations
BAFIA	Banking and Financial Institutions Act
BNM	Bank Negara Malaysia
CDRC	Corporate Debt Restructuring Committee
CEO	chief executive officer
CIC	Capital Issues Committee
CMP	*Capital Market Masterplan*
CMP2	*Capital Market Masterplan 2*
CMSA	Capital Markets and Services Act
D-SIB	domestic systemically important bank
EPF	Employees Provident Fund
FHC	financial holding company
FSA	Financial Services Act
FSBP	*Financial Sector Blueprint*
FSMP	*Financial Sector Masterplan*
GDP	gross domestic product
GLC	government-linked company
GLIC	government-linked investment company
IDEAS	Institute for Democracy and Economic Affairs
IFSA	Islamic Financial Services Act
IMF	International Monetary Fund
IOSCO	International Organization of Securities Commissions
KPI	key performance indicator
KWAP	Kumpulan Wang Persaraan (Diperbadankan) [Retirement Fund Incorporated]

LTAT	Lembaga Tabung Angkatan Tentera [Armed Forces Fund Board]
LTH	Lembaga Tabung Haji [Pilgrimage Fund Board]
MoU	Memorandum of Understanding
NBMC	National Bond Market Committee
NEP	New Economic Policy
NPL	non-performing loan
Pemandu	Performance Management and Delivery Unit
PNB	Permodalan Nasional Berhad
SAC	Shariah Advisory Council
SC	Securities Commission
SEACEN	South East Asian Central Banks Research and Training Centre
SPV	special purpose vehicle
SRI	sustainable and responsible investment
SWF	sovereign wealth fund
UMNO	United Malays National Organisation
WEF	World Economic Forum

1 Introduction

As the 1MDB scandal gained international traction in 2015, it took many commentators and financial analysts by surprise. From the outside, Malaysia had looked very stable. Control of the political system had remained firmly in the hands of the United Malays National Organisation-led Barisan Nasional coalition, most recently reconfirmed in the 2013 general election. The Malaysian economy had seemed to prosper, getting close to achieving the government's target of reaching advanced industrialised country status by the year 2020. The financial bureaucracy was seen as competent and managing the economy prudently, perhaps much more so than its US and UK counterparts, whose failures to rein in the financial sector had been so drastically exposed during the global financial crisis of 2008–2009. Indeed, Malaysia had had a relatively smooth run in the early 2010s. International investors had returned to the country after a decade-long hiatus in the wake of the Asian financial crisis of 1997–1998, during which Malaysia had imposed capital controls. Capital outflows during the 'taper tantrum' of 2013 had been much more muted than in neighbouring Indonesia. In particular, its support for the growing Islamic finance sector had given Malaysia an international reputation for being among the most innovative jurisdictions when it came to emerging market financial policymaking.

At the time of writing, former Prime Minister Najib Razak, 1MDB and the intricate financial webs they wove are under investigation in several countries. This includes in Malaysia itself, after the short-lived Pakatan Harapan government now under the administration of Perikatan Nasional, but also, perhaps most prominently, in the USA. Allegations have been well documented in investigative media reports.[1] They include the use of manipulative bond issuances – deeply implicating US investment bank Goldman Sachs; money laundering through various offshore firms and transactions; and a slate of other charges.[2]

Moreover, investigators have expanded their nets and looked into a greater number of actors and their involvement in the scandal and its concealment.[3] Ultimately, it will be down to the courts in Malaysia and elsewhere to establish the extent of 1MDB's wrongdoings and to mete out justice for those involved. Nevertheless, the 1MDB scandal also cast a shadow on Malaysia's, by many accounts highly successful, track record of financial reform in the wake of the 1997–1998 financial crisis.

This book examines how these two narratives can be reconciled. On the one hand, there is the success story of Malaysia as an innovative and quite effective financial reformer. In this guise, it has been applauded by the international financial community and seen as a role model for other emerging markets to emulate. On the other hand, there is the persistent, if not growing, influence of the government on the economy. Close ties between government and business then serve as the backdrop to the scandalous narrative of Malaysia as a country that struggles to escape money politics and is periodically prone to financial crises and recurring scandals.[4] Of course, both these narratives embrace a certain hyperbole. Nevertheless, they leave us with an important question: how is it that a country can become significantly more financially developed, but associated expectations that this would lessen the influence of the state and result in less political control are far from being met?

To unravel this puzzle, this book critically examines the political economy of financial development in Malaysia. Financial development, in this context, and as I will elaborate in more detail in the next chapter, is understood as a process that involves government and market actors, although the distinction between the two is often not as clear cut as it seems at first glance. I will examine the political economy of financial development along a number of dimensions that are typically considered to be largely technical matters: i) the politics of *financial modernisation*, in particular efforts to consolidate the Malaysian banking sector in the aftermath of the 1997–1998 crisis and their implications, ii) the politics of *financial deepening*, with a focus on capital market development, and last but not least iii) the politics of *financial inclusion*, which will be explored through the lens of the country's rapidly growing Islamic finance sector.

A significant correlate of financial development has been the increasing financialisation of Malaysian capitalism. By this, I mean that the reach of finance has become progressively more pervasive not just in the economy, but also in both polity and society. The financialisation of Malaysian capitalism has thrived on a combination of deeply entrenched state capitalism and selective pro-market reforms. The Malaysian experience clearly demonstrates that financialisation is not just a derivative of market idea(l)s, but that the state plays a constitutive role in shaping financialisation dynamics.

Argument in brief

Financial development, rather than being the predominantly technical issue which it is portrayed as in the mainstream economics and policy literatures, has to be understood as a political process. As such, it represents an amalgamation of competing understandings of good economic management and material preferences of the actors involved. This holds true for Malaysia as it does for many other countries. The state is a crucial agent in the financial development process as it can adjudicate between different ideas and interests. Financial development therefore is not only underpinned by changes in the global economy – or market shifts – but deeply enmeshed with domestic politics and the continuation and contestation of prevalent economic paradigms.

In this sense, the key to unpacking Malaysia's complex financial history is to better understand the ambiguities of financial development and its political nature. Malaysia presents a very intriguing case in that its financial markets are considered to be mature, but political control of the financial system and the economy is nevertheless firmly entrenched. Thus, what we see is neither pervasive state capture, given the technocratic strength and moral authority of the financial authorities, specifically the central bank – Bank Negara Malaysia (BNM) – and the Securities Commission (SC). Nor is it a fully autonomous financial bureaucracy that serves the national interest over particular interests as policymakers have to navigate a complex political-economic terrain. Indeed, the very notion of what constitutes the national interest is subject to fierce contestation in Malaysia. This then results in an increasingly professional and internationally networked financial bureaucracy that nevertheless can be quite powerless in the context of financial scandal and patronage politics.

In the two decades since the Asian crisis of 1997–1998, the Malaysian financial system has undergone significant changes. On the market side, the banking system was consolidated and capital markets have taken on a much more substantial role. Moreover, Islamic finance, still a niche phenomenon in the Malaysian financial system of the mid-1990s, catering largely to the rural population, has become ubiquitous and a major preoccupation for the urban financial elites. On the policy front, financial policymakers have pursued an ambitious agenda of reform aimed at widening and deepening domestic financial markets. The institutional standing of the financial bureaucracy has been strengthened with the granting of statutory independence to Bank Negara Malaysia, consolidated by the *Central Bank of Malaysia Act 2009*. Likewise, the statutory powers of the Securities Commission were enhanced by the *Capital Markets & Services Act 2007*. However, in light of recurrent financial scandals and crises, these substantial developments have been eclipsed by a focus on the nexus between politics and business in the Malaysian political economy.

While emerging trends of the financialisation of Malaysian capitalism could already be discerned on the eve of the regional crisis, in its aftermath this accelerated and intensified, on both economic and political grounds. Indeed, the fallout from the Asian crisis, at least temporarily, made more egregious forms of rent-seeking politically difficult to sustain. This led to a push among the widespread web of beneficiaries and institutions, created over successive phases of Malaysian capitalism as detailed in Chapter 3, to reassert their influence in novel ways. Along these lines, close cooperation between the notionally public and private sectors, in the context of deep domestic pools of capital, is perhaps best understood as a form of state-permeated market economy (Nölke *et al.* 2015, 543–545). So-called government-linked companies (GLCs) and government-linked investment companies (GLICs) have played an important role in this regard, as will be shown.

Until the early 2000s, the acronym GLC would have been more familiar in Singapore than in Malaysia. Indeed, the term was used in Singapore for state enterprises with a commercial bottom line (Ramirez and Tan 2003). In the wake of the Asian crisis, this terminology was increasingly embraced in Malaysia, culminating in the GLC Transformation programme announced in 2004 as I will discuss in more detail in Chapter 3. However, as part of the reconceptualisation of state enterprises as GLCs, another acronym would rise to prominence – that of the GLIC. In this context, GLIC refers to a range of state-linked investors, including pension funds, the national unit trust company and the country's sovereign wealth fund (for more details, see Gomez 2017, 6–9). These GLICs have refashioned themselves as major shareholders of GLCs and institutional investors in the Malaysian political economy, a phenomenon for which Wang (2015), in the context of the Chinese political economy, has coined the notion of the 'shareholding state'. Financialisation thus brings into close alignment state-permeated capitalism and the shareholding state.

In the course of financial development, Malaysian capitalism has moved from an interventionist variety of state capitalism geared towards industrialisation and economic restructuring along ethnic lines to a more marketised form of shareholder state capitalism that embraces financialisation dynamics. This has important analytical implications. Rather than continuing to juxtapose interventionist and liberal policy-making, in this inquiry into the Malaysian political economy, I propose a more open-ended approach that focuses on the interplay of state-interventionist and market-liberal tendencies in shaping the Malaysian financial system (Rethel 2010b; see also Gomez and Lafaye de Micheaux 2017). Ultimately, these dynamics have to be understood as a renegotiation of the relationship between an ethnically stratified state and market, as financial principles have become increasingly imbued within the state apparatus, with political control, rather than economic efficiency being the primary purpose.

Such an approach, then, highlights the dynamic nature of the webs of relationships that underpin financial development, all within Malaysia's distinctive ethnic political economy setting. Moreover, it clearly points to the political nature of financial development in both its internal and external relations. In so doing, it brings the political and socio-economic implications of financial development and its relationship with the financialisation of Malaysian capitalism to the fore. At the same time, as later chapters will show, this shift has been a fundamental means of shoring up political control of the financial system. As a result, in Malaysia, the increasingly professional and internationally well-networked financial bureaucracy has to navigate a complex terrain of interests – of political elites, GLICs and GLCs and private actors – and wider national developmental and ethnicity-inflected socio-economic priorities. In this regard, financialisation dynamics are part and parcel of wider forces of state transformation.

In subjecting the history, practices and politics of financial development in Malaysia to scrutiny, the analysis presented in this book echoes a more profound concern in the political economy literature, namely to better understand the evolving relationship between states and markets. The fact that Malaysia is still a developing nation, although in close reach of graduating to being a high-income country, makes its experience especially intriguing. Indeed, the experience of Malaysia casts a light on the evolving role of the state with regard to broader processes of development and marketisation as they relate specifically to the financial system. In so doing, it challenges the rather simplistic notion that as financial globalisation proceeds, the state recedes and market actors step in to dominate processes and outcomes.

In fact, the Malaysian experience demonstrates how the lines between state and market have become increasingly blurred, with the state incorporating market principles, whilst being a substantial shareholder in some of the country's biggest banks. As such, the relationship between financial globalisation and the state is far from straightforward and is shaped by a range of contextual factors. It is by better understanding the Malaysian story that we can gain valuable insights into other developing countries facing divergent interests between a political class, an emerging or consolidating corporate sector, and social cleavages within the wider public (whether these are ethnic/religious, class or geographical) in a period of extreme financial globalisation.[5]

Outline of the book

In exploring the nexus of financial development and financialisation, this book offers fresh insights into the nature of state-permeated capitalism in Malaysia. The next two chapters provide the conceptual and historical background of this study. Chapter 2 examines key debates surrounding the notion of financial development to illustrate both the ambiguous and political nature of the concept, before it is applied to the context of Malaysia. It will suggest that financial development is best conceptualised as a relational category, constituted through both external and internal relationships. After examining financial development in relation to policy autonomy and the real economy, the chapter moves on to critically interrogating major thrusts of financial reform, from banking sector modernisation to capital market deepening to financial inclusion. Chapter 3 provides an overview of the evolution of the Malaysian political economy, illustrating the impact of different phases on financial policymaking. It briefly introduces key actors in the Malaysian financial policymaking process and sets out the major frameworks within which they operate.

The empirical discussion in Chapters 4 and 5 focuses on financial market reforms specifically, and how they intersect with financialisation dynamics. Chapter 4 examines the banking system as a key constituent of the process. Following a period of bank consolidations in the wake of the Asian crisis, rationalised by the need to make Malaysian banks more competitive, government control over the banking sector actually increased. Through its GLICs, the state is a major shareholder in the banking system. This then has important implications for the incentive structure within which banks operate. However, at the same time, there has been growing interest in so-called value-based intermediation, in which the Islamic banks are to take a leading role. Chapter 5 looks at capital market reforms, including efforts to develop the bond market. Once more, the state can be characterised as an important market actor, both as an issuer of and investor in debt securities, including through its GLICs and GLCs. Nonetheless, a growing number of retail investors have also been attracted to the market and, in so doing, given a boost to the investment management industry. Whilst efforts to deepen and widen capital markets are not only an important aspect of financial development they may also accentuate inequalities of wealth.

In concluding, Chapter 6 re-examines the political and socio-economic implications of financial development. It will highlight that in Malaysia, financial development has taken place in the context of a combination of state intervention and selected market-liberal reforms. In so doing, it has contributed to the consolidation of state control of the financial sector, rather than reducing state involvement. At the same time, financial development has accentuated financialisation dynamics in both the banking sector and capital markets. The Malaysian experience also holds important lessons for the design of financial reforms that achieve broader socio-economic progress, and not just for the betterment of small groups of well-connected elites.

Notes

1 See, for example, Gunasegaram and KiniBiz (2018) and Rewcastle Brown (2018) for book-length accounts that are more journalistic in style.
2 For a summary, see e.g. *The Edge* (18 December 2019); *New Straits Times* (26 July 2020).
3 *The Edge* (8 January 2019); *The Edge* (22 June 2020).
4 For a recent commentary, see the *Malay Mail* (2 June 2020).
5 I am grateful to one of the reviewers for highlighting this point.

2   The politics of financial development

The notion of financial development first gained traction in the 1950s in work that focused on the relationship between the structure of the financial system and national economic growth (Goldsmith 1959). With regard to developing countries, a particular focus was on the impact of financial system configurations on capital formation (Hirschman 1958). The idea of financial development gained a new lease of life in the wake of the emerging market financial crises of the late 1990s and early 2000s. In response to the havoc brought about by these crises, there was agreement on a broad front that, first, there was a role for the state in ensuring the stability of the financial system and that, second, the development of national financial systems was a crucial component of international financial stability (Rethel 2010a). To this effect, financial stability and the orderly development of financial systems were increasingly understood to be public goods, requiring state action. The financial development agenda was reinforced by academic research that pointed to the importance of better understanding the relationship between financial development, economic growth and risk (e.g. Levine 1997; Allen and Gale 2001).

Nevertheless, some authors have pointed out that financial development, far from being a unidirectional process, historically has been subject to 'great reversals' (Rajan and Zingales 2003). Indeed, on a systemic level, questions were raised about whether financial development had 'made the world riskier' (Rajan 2005; 2011). Whilst these doubts were largely ignored in the exuberance that characterised the period in the run up to the global financial crisis of 2008–2009, the 2008 crisis brought vulnerabilities caused by financial (over)development home with a vengeance. Moreover, despite the idea of financial development gaining widespread support, significant cross-national variation persists across financial systems, including in Southeast Asia (see e.g. Pepinsky 2012; Rethel 2014). One of the key expectations from progressive financial development, leaving aside for now the rather tricky question of how exactly a developed financial system is supposed to look like, is that credit mobilisation, intermediation and allocation become more efficient, often with the implicit assumption that this would also reduce opportunities for rent-seeking. And yet, recent financial scandals and crises, in Malaysia and elsewhere, hardly support such a supposition.[1] Indeed, there is some evidence that financial development actually has contributed to reduced efficiency, at least in Southeast Asian banking systems (Subramaniam *et al.* 2019). Thus, financial development is actually a rather ambiguous concept that gives significant interpretative leeway to government and market actors. However, focusing on financial inclusion, Dafe (2020) shows that this ambiguity can in fact be constructive in that it creates room for developing country agency and we will see this play out in the case of Malaysia, too, in later chapters, and with reference to Islamic finance in particular.

The next section will explore the idea of financial development and the discourses that surround it in more depth. It will suggest that to better understand the contested nature of financial development, we have to treat it as a relational category. The remainder of this chapter then looks at financial development in both its external and internal relations. It will examine financial development in the context of policy autonomy and the so-called real economy on the one hand, and financial development and the modernisation and deepening of financial systems as well as financial inclusion on the other hand. It will highlight that the nature of these relationships is informed by competing normative and material preferences and interests.

Financial development in theory and practice

Since the emerging market financial crises of the 1990s and early 2000s, there has been a growing intellectual consensus around the importance of financial development for financial stability and economic prosperity. Albeit with varying success rates, this consensus has been accompanied by a proliferation of national, regional and transnational planning exercises, assessment schemes and data transparency initiatives, all geared towards the development and evaluation of financial systems. However, as I will show in this section, these approaches tend to underestimate the relational character of financial development by ignoring the dense webs of relationships that underpin it.

Financial development as relational category

Financial development planning is widespread in Southeast Asia. This includes, for example, various national financial sector planning exercises and development plans in countries ranging from Malaysia to Indonesia to Thailand (see e.g. Bank Negara Malaysia 2001; 2011; Bank of Thailand 2006; Otoritas Jasa Keuangan 2016). Moreover, a number of regional-level initiatives have been undertaken under the auspices of the ASEAN Capital Markets Forum (ACMF) and the ASEAN Central Bank Governors (see e.g. ACMF 2016).[2] With regard to evaluation exercises, perhaps the most famous are the Financial Sector Assessment Programs (FSAPs), conducted jointly by IMF and World Bank. However, in Southeast Asia these are complemented by a number of national and regional initiatives, such as the ASEAN Corporate Governance Scorecard (Asian Development Bank and ASEAN Capital Market Forum 2017). Likewise, there have been considerable efforts to improve the availability of data to assess and measure financial development. The best known of these initiatives are the World Bank's *Financial Development and Structure Database* and its *Global Financial Development Database* (Beck *et al.* 1999; Čihák *et al.* 2012). At the regional level, information on the development of bond markets specifically is provided by the ADB-hosted platform *AsianBondsOnline*.

With the greater availability of data, there have been attempts to create indices and benchmarks that rank countries according to the development of their financial systems. These exercises are conducted by both public bodies and private entities and serve as reference points in development plans. Thus, for example, the World Economic Forum (WEF), widely known for its *Global Competitiveness Reports*, also used to compile *Financial Development Reports*, espousing a similar logic of country ranking. Table 2.1 provides a snapshot of how the *Financial Development Report* ranks Southeast Asian financial systems in both regional and global perspective. This snapshot sees Singapore, as the financially most developed Southeast Asian country, ranked at place 4 (out of 60 countries and after Hong Kong, the US and the UK) and Malaysia somewhere in the top third at place 18 (World Economic Forum 2012, 13). The WEF initiative ultimately was rather short-lived – the report was published annually between 2008 and 2012. Nevertheless, the economic, political and social significance of such efforts should not be ignored for at least three reasons.

First, these indicators and indices provide snapshot overviews of financial systems that developed over decades if not centuries (Verdier 2002). In so doing by necessity, they brush over political, economic

Table 2.1 Southeast Asia in the WEF Financial Development Index

Overall	Institutional Environment	Business Environment	Financial Stability	Banking Financial Services	Non-Bank Financial Services	Financial Markets	Financial Access
4-SG	1-SG	1-SG	3-SG	10-SG	12-SG	3-SG	14-SG
18-MY	21-MY	25-MY	10-MY	11-MY	14-MY	24-MY	25-TH
34-TH	33-TH	45-TH	34-TH	28-TH	21-PH	33-TH	28-MY
49-PH	39-PH	53-ID	35-ID	32-VN	23-ID	34-PH	43-VN
50-ID	51-ID	54-PH	47-PH	36-PH	42-TH	37-VN	53-PH
52-VN	53-VN	56-VN	56-VN	53-ID	51-VN	54-ID	55-ID

Source: World Economic Forum (2012, 13–14)
Notes: Singapore = SG, Malaysia = MY, Thailand = TH, Indonesia = ID, Philippines = PH and Vietnam = VN

and cultural dynamics that were instrumental in shaping how a specific financial system developed, and without understanding which analyses of the operation of any given financial system are always rather limited. For example, Pepinsky (2012) draws attention to the role of historical political exigencies in shaping financial development in Southeast Asia. Indeed, while it is possible to track how countries slide up and down in these annual rankings, it is highly questionable how much financial systems really change in a short span of time and how much explanatory value can be attributed to single factors. Despite these caveats, financial development indicators and rankings can nevertheless draw attention to variations in how financial systems develop and change. This does neither mean that trajectories of financial development follow an inevitably economic logic nor that these patterns are irreversible (Rajan and Zingales 2003).

Second, the very meaning of these indices and benchmarks is often unclear. The global financial crisis has starkly demonstrated that financial development or, more accurately, obtaining a high overall score in this type of index does not mean that a financial system is crisis-proof. Both the UK and the US financial system are typically deemed to be very developed, yet they were at the core of the 2008–2009 global financial crisis – and have been sources of global systemic instabilities both prior to and since then.[3] Moreover, the composition of these indicators also clearly reflects the political and social values that are attached to them. In this regard, so-called 'financial inclusion' measures such as number of bank accounts as a share of the overall population have become increasingly popular, but they say very little about what it is that the target populations are included in. As we will see below in the section on financial development and the real economy, it clearly matters if a financial system is geared towards financing productive capacity or if it mainly serves the ultimately unsustainable accumulation of debt. Thus, the financial categories employed in these studies are by far not as politically unambiguous as the rather technical language indicates, in which they are described.

On their own, the two previous points about the nature of these benchmarks and indicators probably would matter very little; financial development indicators would just join a huge slew of other measures that are never much put to use. However, and third, these sorts of rankings are performative in the sense that policymakers use them to benchmark their own ambitions against them (see e.g. Broome and Quirk 2015; Broome *et al.* 2018). Thus, for example, the WEF Index features in the second Malaysian *Capital Market Masterplan*, covering the period from 2011 to 2020. More specifically, it is used to demonstrate that the Malaysian stock market 'ranks highly' with regard to access to financing (Securities Commission 2011, 2). But this then makes financial policymaking very much subject to what Jeffrey Chwieroth (2014), in the context of sovereign wealth fund creation, has described as 'fads and fashions'. Arguably, a lot of the efforts to develop bond markets in emerging and frontier economies from the late 1990s crises until at least the global financial crisis of 2008 espoused a similar logic. This was despite important interventions, most famously perhaps by then World Bank chief economist Justin Lin Yifu, who argued that the greater capital market orientation of advanced industrialised countries might not necessarily suit developing economies' needs (Lin *et al.* 2009).

Looking back more than two decades after the Asian financial crisis, and from the vantage points of more recent crises originating both in the financial and real economies, it becomes clear that Malaysian financial elites used the crisis of 1997–1998 to engineer sweeping reforms to the financial system. As a result, the banking system became more concentrated and the role of capital markets, specifically of bond markets, as a source of funds increased substantially. More generally, capital markets now play a more salient role in the economy. Indeed, at first glance, Malaysia's financial structure increasingly resembles the capital market-based financial systems of the US and the UK. At the same time, however, so-called 'government-linked' entities play a significant role in the provision of both financial capital and market expertise, which only serves to indicate that conceptual frameworks and categories – such as state and market, public and private – do not travel easily across financial and economic systems. It therefore makes sense to adopt a more relational approach to understanding financial development. This does not so much eradicate the ambiguities that notions of financial development entail as that it embraces them in an analytically and empirically productive manner, recognising the inherently political nature of financial development in theory and practice.

Rather than thinking about it in absolute terms, i.e. a country is either financially developed or not, I suggest considering financial development as a relational category that structures various aspects of the economy. Cognitive psychologist Dedre Gentner (2005, 245) defines relational categories as 'categories whose meanings consist either of (a) relations with other entities [or dynamics ...], or (b) internal relations among a set of components'. For the case of financial development, I will illustrate in the remainder of this chapter how it is shaped by both external and internal relations. In the following two subsections, I will briefly discuss two of the external dynamics that are of particular relevance to the notion of financial development: the relationship between financial development and the so-called real economy; and its relevance for notions of policy autonomy, both domestically and internationally. This will be followed, in turn, by a discussion of internal dynamics, more specifically with regard to the banking system and capital markets along the three dimensions of financial modernisation, financial deepening and financial inclusion.

Financial development and policy autonomy

Policy autonomy can be defined either in the negative as being 'free from' certain political and economic actors and influences or in the positive as the 'capacity to' formulate and implement policies. In either definition, it has both domestic and international dimensions. Let me explore in more detail what this means. The dominant view of policy autonomy adopts a negative definition. This is clearly reflected, for example, in the literature on central banks. A core focus of that literature is the question of the extent to which financial authorities – primarily central banks, but in some instances also securities commissions, are insulated from what is typically perceived as undue political influence. A common measure in this regard would be central bank independence, with great weight being given to statutory provisions, i.e. legal independence. In general terms, the period since the Asian financial crisis of the late 1990s has seen a move towards greater central bank independence around the world (Marcussen 2007). However, such an approach significantly underappreciates the role played by other factors in the precise configuration of a given political economy. Thus, for example, statutory independence is a relative concept in a political culture where social hierarchies are important and strong deference is paid to political leaders; witness for example the tribal politics of the Trump administration in the US where (perceived) loyalty literally trumps competence. Therefore, whilst statutory provisions for policy autonomy might give financial authorities a certain degree of leverage, political culture and relationships matter.

A similar understanding of policy autonomy – defining it as the opposite of being (unduly) influenced by economic and political interests – underpins much of the work on regulatory capture (Young 2012). In particular since the global financial crisis of 2008, there has been much interest in the opportunities for and scope and pace of financial sector reforms, targeting a range of often closely interrelated issues such as excessive risk-taking, bonus culture, the rise of shadow-banking or socially harmful financial innovation (Rethel and Sinclair 2012; Moschella and Tsingou 2013). Regulatory capture operates as a continuum, bookended by the close alignment of regulatory and other interests on the one end and financial regulators virtually being taken hostage by powerful economic and political interests on the other. In reality, most forms of regulatory capture fall somewhere in between. Thus, regulatory interests can be closely aligned with those of politicians and/or business, for example to maintain regime stability or because of groupthink as in the case of executive compensation in an age of 'talent'. Once more, there exist a range of statutory responses that can be undertaken to address (at least some forms of) regulatory capture, including legal protections of regulators and measures to slow down or close revolving doors between financial regulation and politics and business. For instance, Khan (2018) analyses the greater use of immunity, liability limiting and indemnity instruments by central banks at a time when their mandates have expanded to playing a greater role in financial supervision. Similarly, there have been considerations of slowing down or even closing the revolving door between politics, regulators and business, for example by requiring extended periods of 'gardening leave' or reforming regulatory and corporate appointment systems.

Another dimension of policy autonomy emphasises the impact of globalisation on nation states and their policy choices (Nelson 1990; Nelson *et al.* 2008). International financial institutions and international investors are but two groups of actors often cited as impacting on national government's 'room to move' (Mosley 2000). There has been much debate on whether globalisation weakens the nation-state vis-à-vis these international economic forces. Other work has drawn attention to how a broader array of actors ranging from rating agencies to international law firms to index providers impacts policy space (for example, Sinclair 2005; Faulconbridge 2019; Petry *et al.* 2019). However, it has also brought much needed nuance to the debate. Thus, for instance Mosley suggests that investors typically take their cue from only a rather limited number of signals (2000; 2003). Similarly, domestic pools of investment that can be strategically deployed as investors-of-last resort at times of market stress can provide some autonomy from global financial cycles, but may also increase rent-seeking behaviour. Once again, relationships – and how they develop over time – clearly matter.

The experience of Malaysia is a case in point. Thus, for example, Malaysia has been seeking to cultivate relationships with international bond investors since the early 1980s when it began issuing sovereign bonds in a range of currencies (Singh 1984). Similarly, in the wake of the Asian crisis, Malaysian financial regulators have sought to increase their 'voice' in international financial networks (Securities Commission 2001, 18). Indeed, forging such close relations with the international financial community has been particularly important in the case of Islamic finance. The by now widespread recognition of *sukuk* – Islamic finance instruments akin to bonds – as a distinct asset class has been the result of sustained efforts by the Malaysian authorities to cultivate relations with investors and capital market-supporting institutions such as credit rating agencies and educate them about the characteristics of these instruments (Lai *et al.* 2017).

By necessity, this discussion of policy autonomy has been a broad sweep, brushing over differences between types of policy autonomy – such as monetary, regulatory or fiscal autonomy, a focus on each of which brings to the fore somewhat different webs of relationships. Nevertheless, it clearly demonstrates the importance of taking into account such relationships when it comes to understanding and analysing financial development – including relations between politicians and regulators, between business and politics, and between regulators and business. This more relational aspect of policymaking has been recognised in particular in the 'developmental state' literature, including in the work of Peter Evans (1995) on 'embedded autonomy' and Linda Weiss (1998) on 'governed interdependence'. Here, a positive definition of autonomy as 'capacity-to' is employed (e.g. Weiss 1998, Chapter 3). On this reading, states, and agencies within the state such as economic ministries, can derive significant clout to shape industrial transformation from how they manage and nurture their relations with business. This approach emphasises not so much the coercive power of the state, but forms of moral suasion, cultivating relationships, and networked governance, including at the regional and international level (Nesadurai 2011; Jones and Zeitz 2019). Therefore, both domestic political economy and international regulatory context are important in understanding how capacity-to manifests itself.

However, what is less clear-cut is how this capacity-to translates into effective policymaking specifically in the case of financial development. Indeed, finance is typically seen as a prop, rather than a target of states' transformative will (Rethel 2020). This is problematic for a number of reasons, in particular the pervasive impact on national development and socio-economic welfare especially in cases where and when finance, and the relationships that underpin it, turn toxic. In the short term, this can result in financial instability and crisis. In the long term, it can contribute to socially suboptimal financialisation. A crucial component in this, I would argue, is the relationship between financial development and the so-called 'real' economy which I will examine next.

Financial development and the real economy

The cornerstone of the developmental state system of the state-led pursuit of economic growth was a bank-based financial system (Öniş 1991). In the late-industrialising Asian economies, including to some extent in Malaysia, financial repression was used as a deliberate development strategy to pursue economic growth. Selective credit programmes directed funds to sectors and industries which governments identified as important for their countries' economic transformation. Financing choices tended to be in favour of bank debt rather than equity, with financial systems characteristically being little diversified. Banks provided the capital necessary for development. In return, the state safeguarded the interests of the banks and imposed, for instance, high barriers to entry (Haggard and Lee 1993).

This model was based on the premise that short-term market logic would not generate the required long-term investment necessary for industrialisation. Therefore, there was a role for government to channel investment to targeted sectors and industries seen as crucial to bringing about economic transformation. One such mechanisms was to get prices 'wrong' on purpose as the allocation of capital did not necessarily follow a (short-term) market logic (Amsden 1989). Nevertheless, financing was clearly geared towards big business, which also was better able to generate funds internally. In addition, risk was very concentrated which made this model of 'indebted industrialisation' highly vulnerable to shocks (Bowie and Unger 1997, 13; see also Wade and Veneroso 1998). It relied on insulation from the world economy, for example through capital controls.

In this model, the capital needs of both households and small enterprises were seen as subordinate to the overarching goal of national economic growth. Finance was subordinated to the needs of the 'real', industrial economy and financial development designed to serve industrial strategy. As Wade (2004, 27) points out, a key feature of the developmental state was its control over the financial system, 'making private financial capital subordinate to industrial capital'. In Malaysia, as in many other developing countries, this entailed a two-step process: addressing foreign control of the financial system, and reorienting it towards the financing of (nascent) domestic industries. A distinctive characteristic in this regard was that Malaysia also sought to redistribute corporate ownership along ethnic lines, as I will discuss in more detail in the next chapter.

Much has happened since the heydays of the developmental state, especially so in the world of finance. The end of the Bretton Woods system of capital controls and fixed exchange rates in the 1970s set in motion a range of changes whose repercussions were felt around the globe. It was followed, in short order, by the liberalisation of interest rates, a significant surge in private lending to developing countries and, almost inevitably, a series of financial crises. Rather than financing industrial transformation in the Global South, international finance became increasingly speculative in nature, leading the eminent political economist Susan Strange (1986) to characterise it as a system of 'casino capitalism'. Yet another change was underway that was to become more visible at the turn of the century, and that was the advance of financialisation, defined by Epstein (2019, 380) as 'the increasing importance of financial markets, financial motives, financial institutions, and financial elites in the operations of the economy and its governing institutions, both at the national and international levels'.

Whilst the early financialisation literature focused very much on the experience of advanced industrialised countries, in particular that of the US, more recently attention has shifted to financialisation in developing and emerging market economies such as Malaysia (see e.g. Rethel 2010b; Bonizzi 2013; Bortz and Kaltenbrunner 2018). In so doing, it has also sparked a growing body of scholarship that explores processes of state financialisation, understood as financialisation of the state itself rather than by the state (Datz 2008; Wang 2015). Indeed, financialisation is a multi-faceted phenomenon, impacting not just macro-economic dynamics, but also touching down in a growing number of areas of daily life (Martin 2002). For the purposes of this book, I will focus on the aspect of financialisation that foregrounds the changing relationship between the financial and real – or productive – economy, in favour of the former.[4] Indeed, this is an understanding of financialisation that has also been embraced by Malaysian financial regulators. Thus, the Securities Commission states in its second *Capital Market Masterplan*,

> While financial innovation has channelled greater flows of capital into financing innovation and enterprise, it has also increased the financialisation of economic activities relative to the generation of productive wealth. The rising proportion of financial assets relative to physical assets is a phenomenon arising from the globalisation of financial markets as well as the expanding role of intangible assets in creating wealth.
>
> (Securities Commission 2011, 13)

In particular, work examining the economics of financialisation has made significant progress in looking in more detail at how financial development affects, for example, the allocation of capital across economic sectors and what this means in terms of the development (or not) of productive capacity on the one hand, and the level of property and other asset prices on the other (e.g. Karwowski and Stockhammer 2017). Some of this work has looked specifically at the impact of the growth and institutionalisation of capital markets (e.g. Rethel 2010b). At the same time, there has been a growing recognition that the financial sector also operates as a real sector in that it generates employment and income. For example, in 2018, employment in the Malaysian financial services sector stood at more than 165,000 people according to central bank figures.[5] It is open for debate how much of this presents a brain drain from the real economy.[6]

In this context, the Malaysian experience is particularly illuminating in that the country has been at the forefront of promoting Islamic finance as an alternative financial system that emphasises investment in 'productive economic activities' (e.g. Zeti 2009). Based on the teachings of Islam, Islamic finance represents a principled approach to finance. It is shaped by both prohibitions and requirements, in order to promote the *maqasid al-sharia*, the foundational goals of Islamic jurisprudence: protection of faith, life, progeny, intellect and property. Thus, Islamic prohibitions include: the paying and receiving of *riba* (interest) and engaging in *maisir* (gambling) and *gharar* (contractual ambiguity). In so doing, Islamic finance takes issue with the asymmetric transfer of risk, where one party gains at the cost of another, often through speculative activities. Instead, Islamic finance emphasises risk-sharing and the need for economic reward to be associated with tangible contributions to the economy. This is promoted by the requirement of linking financial transaction to real assets and/or economic effort. Nevertheless, the growth of Islamic finance in Malaysia cannot be disentangled from financialisation dynamics, including the shift towards household lending and rising levels of household debt (Rethel 2016).

Bortz and Kaltenbrunner (2018) draw attention to the impact of currency hierarchies on financialisation dynamics in emerging economies. More specifically, they suggest that dependence on external currencies, primarily the US dollar, exacerbates the volatility of capital flows to emerging economies, impacting asset prices and the transmission of shocks. As an oil exporting country, Malaysia is somewhat less at risk of a shortfall of US dollar reserves. Indeed, Malaysia's national oil company, Petronas, makes a significant contribution to the budget, both in terms of tax revenue and by paying an annual dividend to the government. In 2019, this dividend amounted to RM54 billion, including an RM30 billion special dividend to address a widening government deficit.[7]

At the same time, Malaysia remains exposed to volatile international capital flows, and its policy stance in this regard has been oscillating between interventionism and liberalisation. For example, there was a sustained drop in foreign holdings of domestic government bonds and sukuk, including shorter-term paper, from a peak of 36 per cent of all holdings in September 2016 to a trough of 26 per cent in March 2017.[8] One policy measure taken by Bank Negara Malaysia was to require exporters to convert at least 75 per cent of their export proceeds into Malaysian ringgit. Conversely, in 2018, Bank Negara introduced new measures liberalising the management of foreign currency receipts and facilitating the hedging of foreign currency obligations.[9] Efforts to liberalise the foreign exchange regime were ratcheted up further in 2019, also following conversations with global bond index provider FT Russell, which had put Malaysia on its watch list.[10] In so doing, questions of policy autonomy and financialisation seem to become increasingly interconnected.

The salience of finance is one of the most remarkable aspects of present day capitalisms. What is at stake here is a fundamental transformation of the economy. Systemic reconfigurations of the relationship between the real and financial economies – and the growing interconnectedness between the two – have been integral parts of financial development. In this regard, it is important to heed Pike and Pollard's (2010) caution that one should not follow the temptation to see this as a disconnect between real and financial economies, but new entanglements between the two. The experience of Malaysia offers important lessons in this regard as later chapters will show. But first let us examine the contentious politics of financial development by examining its internal relations, with a focus on banking systems and capital markets.

Financial development as politics

Understanding financial development as a relational category allows us to see it as a historically contingent process, comprised of a range of socio-political phenomena that do not fit a one-size-fits-all approach. Moreover, there exist significant differences between financial development as it is theoretically conceived, and how it unfolds on the ground. Thus, on the one hand, in much of the public discourse, financial development is characterised by abstract knowledge claims, technical jargon and bureaucratic processes that to a large extent pre-empt democratic engagement. The use of buzzwords such as financial modernisation, financial deepening or financial inclusion is a case in point – they obfuscate, rather than elucidate. In the remainder of this chapter I will highlight some of the contentious politics that they obscure. In so doing, I will discuss general dynamics that financial systems have been subject to over the last three decades. Nevertheless, it is imperative to point out right from the outset that their relative importance and causal impact in Malaysia is far from straightforward as later chapters will illustrate.

The politics of financial modernisation

For much of the post-World War II period, states around the world retained a tight control over the activities that financial institutions could pursue. In the wake of the demise of the Bretton Woods system in the 1970s, these controls were dismantled and their protections eroded, all under the mantle of financial modernisation. A key moment in this regard was the 1999 Financial Services Modernization Act (also known after its proposers as the Gramm–Leach–Bliley Act) in the US that repealed separations between commercial and investment banking that dated back to the Glass-Stegall Act of 1933 in support of the creation of big financial holding groups. It marked a period in which banking systems around the world, including in Malaysia, underwent a number of significant transformations: a shift towards universal banking, greater concentration of credit intermediation and a push for internationalisation as banks increasingly sought to extend their reach beyond their historical home markets.

First, changes in financial system patterns indicate a significant shift towards universal banking (Crockett *et al.* 2003). Different types of financial institutions, such as commercial banks, finance companies and merchant banks all were consolidated within big financial conglomerates. Whilst universal banking ostensibly had for long been popular in countries such as Germany, the fusion of commercial and investment banking operations – and the growing weight given to the latter – was unprecedented. The perhaps most famous exercise in this regard was the acquisition of Bankers Trust by Deutsche Bank in 1998, with the aim of strengthening Deutsche's investment banking arm (Rethel and Sinclair 2012).

In Malaysia, the consolidation of the banking system in the wake of the 1997–1998 crisis also contributed to the emergence of large banking groups as I will discuss in more detail in Chapter 4. Similarly, Malaysian banks pursued strategic regional acquisitions, among other things to strengthen their investment banking operations. Take, for example, Maybank's acquisition of a 44.6 per cent stake in Singapore-based investment bank Kim Eng in 2011 or CIMB's acquisition of

Singapore-based GK Goh Securities in 2005, and in 2011 of much of the investment banking businesses of the Royal Bank of Scotland as well as of SICCO Securities, a Thai stockbroking company.[11] Nevertheless, perhaps even more important has been a significant expansion in retail banking (Ertürk and Solari 2007). Similarly, in Malaysia, there has also been a significant change in banks' loan portfolios geared toward an increase in household lending (Bank Negara Malaysia 2011, 55).

Second, and closely related, there was a shift towards a greater concentration of credit intermediation in many countries around the world, indicated by measures such as the rising share of total assets of the three biggest banks.[12] This greater concentration of credit intermediation is most obvious in banking systems that underwent consolidation, such as Malaysia and Singapore in the wake of the Asian financial crisis of the late 1990s (Cook 2008). However, it can also be observed in more fragmented banking systems, such as Indonesia, where observers focusing on the sheer number of banks tend to overlook that, in effect, a relatively small number of banks provide a majority of loans. In Malaysia, in the period from 1999 to 2006, bank concentration more than doubled as I will discuss in more detail in Chapter 4, before declining again following the introduction of financial liberalisation measures (see also Figure 4.1 in Chapter 4).

Third, there has been a trend towards the greater regionalisation and/ or internationalisation of banks. Once more, this is closely linked to, but nevertheless analytically distinct from the shift towards universal banking and changes in the pattern of credit intermediation. Indeed, the ambition of making domestic banks more competitive internationally, in particular in the context of sinking margins at home, was one of the major factors underpinning consolidation. As a consequence, not only has there been a greater number of Asian banks among the world's biggest banks as Table 2.2 indicates, but they are also increasingly internationally active. Along these lines, a number of Malaysian banks have strengthened their presence in particular in the ASEAN and Greater China region.

Despite these common patterns, there remains significant variation in how they play out in specific country contexts. For example, whilst the consolidation of the banking system in the aftermath of the Asian crisis was government-led in Malaysia, as I will discuss in more detail in Chapter 4, in other contexts, pressure has come from shareholders keen on consolidating their positions. This is a trend we are likely to see accelerating once more in the aftermath of the COVID-19 pandemic. Nevertheless, what should be clear is that financial modernisation is far from being the dry technocratic exercise as that it is usually portrayed. It

Table 2.2 The world's 1,000 biggest banks by region of origin, 2000–2020

	2000	2010	2020
Europe	388	319	264
US/North America*	199	169	198
Middle East	77	90	68
Latin America	50	44	51
Asia	266	321	376
Rest of World	20	57	43

Source: Timewell (2010)/ *The Banker*; Kemplay (2020)/ *The Banker*
Note: *2020 data aggregates US in North America

reflects distinctive combinations of normative preferences, for example with regard to ideas about national and international competitiveness, and material interests as well as the context-contingent constraints on and opportunities for their realisation.

The politics of financial deepening

In the wake of the emerging market financial crises of the late 1990s and early 2000s, the notion of financial deepening drew greater attention to the development of domestic capital markets. In particular, efforts to develop domestic bond markets were seen as an important means of diversifying financial systems and strengthening their resilience. This was based on the idea of equipping them with a 'spare tire', the lack of which had been a common diagnosis of the financial fallout from the Asian crisis (see Rethel 2010a). Closely related, the period also saw greater interest in the role of non-bank financial institutions in overall financial development (Carmichael and Pomerleano 2002). This contributed to further changes in financial systems, more specifically an acceleration and intensification of financial disintermediation, and closely related a shortening of time horizons and changing attitudes towards leverage and risk. Let me explore these concepts in turn.

In the period following the demise of the Bretton Woods system, financial disintermediation gathered pace. It moved from the advanced industrialised countries, supported, for example, by 'big bang' reforms in the UK and Japan in the mid-1980s, to the so-called developing and emerging markets. The Malaysian experience is rather distinctive in this regard. Here, from the 1970s onwards, a focus on corporate restructurings, a distinct feature of Malaysia's ethnically stratified capitalism as the next chapter will show, had given the stock market and the merchant banking industry a significant boost (Singh 1984, 316).[13] Efforts to develop the domestic bond market date to the mid-1980s and the country's growing emphasis on privatisation. Taken together, these developments make Malaysia rather unique in that its capital markets already were very prominent at a time when it was still very much a developing country. Nevertheless, in the wake of the Asian crisis, the development of capital markets gained further momentum as I will discuss in Chapter 5.

A major feature of many arm's-length capital markets is the shortening time horizon, namely the relative increase in importance of short-term profit maximisation to drive up shareholder value vis-à-vis long-term investment in productive capacity. In other words, progressive financial disintermediation is seen to foster the displacement of a diachronic logic of investment, where financial activity is linked to the investment in productive assets, by a synchronic investment logic 'concerned with the short term and with the profits that can be accumulated in financial markets' (Sinclair 2005, 58–59; see also Rethel and Sinclair 2012). Some accounts have drawn attention to changes in investor profiles as potentially mitigating effects, specifically with regard to the rise of so-called 'patient capital', including investors such as pension funds that favour longer engagements (Deeg and Hardie 2016). Whilst Malaysian capital markets are indeed dominated by pension funds and other government-linked investors, because of political exigencies, when it comes to performance their time horizons are rather short-term. The distinctive type of state-permeated capitalism that exists in Malaysia is heavily reliant on dividends, which are seen as important to guaranteeing political stability as I will discuss in more detail in the next chapter (see also Pepinsky 2008, 247).

Moreover, with the greater prominence of capital markets also come changing attitudes towards leverage and risk. In the ideal-typical banking model, the bank takes on lending risk on the investors' behalf. To minimise this risk, banks screen and monitor the loans they extend. In a capital market-based financial system, complex lending decisions are by and large reduced to judgements about the creditworthiness of the borrower. Securities markets allow for the separation between investment (capital) and risk. Only limited control exists once funds are disbursed. As a consequence, efforts to mitigate risk become disproportionately important. According to the model, while the financing of economic activity is at the core in a bank-based financial system, it is the management of risk in a securitised economy. However, once more there exist significant differences in the Malaysian case. Perhaps one of the most important of these is that investment banks are part of larger banking groups, meaning that effectively banking institutions are actively participating in their own disintermediation. Moreover, with memories of the late 1990s crisis still fresh, risk appetite is somewhat curtailed, leading for example to a concentration of bond investments in the high investment grade categories.

The picture is rather more mixed when it comes to leverage. In arm's-length markets, creditor relations tend to be underpinned by a debt repayment norm 'in that placing a priority on repaying debt is morally right and obligatory' (Sinclair 2005, 66). However, this contrasts starkly with the frowning upon debt finance that was common, for example, in medieval Europe and which is a driving force of the current resurgence of Islamic finance (Warde 2000). The expansion of bond finance further entrenches a change in the perception of debt in favour of seeing it as a legitimate source of profit that in turn has entailed a more fundamental shift in financial culture. However, in Malaysia such a narrative is contested and serves as an important rationale for the development of Islamic financial instruments such as sukuk (Rudnyckyj 2019).

Once more, subjecting the technical language of financial reform to closer scrutiny makes visible political dynamics that underpin it. As such, financial development entails socio-economic consequences that reach far beyond its primary financial sector target. Indeed, such a wider understanding of financial development as social engineering is partially embraced by the concept of financial inclusion to which I turn next.

The politics of financial inclusion

In the wake of the global financial crisis of 2008–2009, financial inclusion has become something of a buzzword in global development circles (Dafe 2020). Increasingly, financial inclusion is seen as a near panacea to a whole plethora of development challenges – poverty alleviation, reducing inequality and women's empowerment to name but a few. By their very nature financial inclusion projects are inherently political – their underlying rationale is to change who has access to what forms of credit and under what conditions. At the same time, the promotion of the financial inclusion agenda rather paradoxically relies on several sleight of hand moves to create a distinctive image of financial exclusion in the first place, as a problem that can be addressed. Financial exclusion is a multi-scalar and multi-faceted phenomenon that plays out very differently in different countries. However, typical financial inclusion strategies share common traits such as a prioritisation of formal financial services and for-profit finance. At the same time, much less attention has been paid to how financial development might further accentuate inequalities of wealth.

Financial inclusion agendas are very much oriented towards access to formal financial services and use indicators such as individual and corporate access to bank accounts as measures of success. In so doing, rather than addressing the causes of financial inequality, such as lack of income, they focus on the consequences. Thus, for example, the Malaysian central bank suggests that '[f]inancial inclusion would include the general public having access to financing, financial services, financial redress and financial information' (Bank Negara Malaysia, no date). But what is the purpose of this financial inclusion? Indeed, financial inclusion often comes hand in hand with greater individual financial responsibilisation. Thus, a major rationale for the implementation of various financial inclusion schemes is that they will better enable target populations to prepare and provide for life risks – children's education, ill health, old age. However, this then very much presumes that – rather than being public or social goods – education, health care and old age provision are private goods to be purchased by individuals in the market place rather than provided by families and/or communities and/ or the state. As a consequence, financial development might actually contribute to widening inequalities of opportunity and wealth, between the 'haves' and the 'have nots'.

Closely related is the greater prioritisation of for-profit finance. Whilst making bank accounts available at no or little cost has been an important thrust in the financial inclusion agenda, restrictions tend to be in place related to who actually is eligible for these accounts. Moreover, together with the emphasis on formal financial services, we see the erosion of alternative financing arrangements. In the process, the financial inclusion agenda has become significantly entangled with dynamics of financialisation. Islamic finance is a case in point. It has not been immune to financialisation, although it potentially offers resources and strategies to mitigate and resist it. The most prominent of these would be the not-for-profit concept of *qard al hasan* or benevolent loan. Instead, the link to the real economy has led to a significant exposure to property which can be deeply problematic, given the correlation of financialisation with asset price inflation and the risk of property bubbles in more financialised financial systems. There is also a tendency in Islamic finance to design products that mirror existing conventional financial products, with a lot of emphasis on personal and consumer finance. Whilst Islamic finance has both a commercial and a charitable dimension, there has been a tendency to link the two via fee-based activities, which demarcates in an increasingly narrow manner the possibility to think finance differently.

Financial inclusion has joined the ranks of earlier policy thrusts such as financial modernisation and financial deepening. Nevertheless, it is yet another term that obscures much of the politics in which it is grounded, in terms of both the relationships that underpin it and the values and material interests that inform it. Making some of those fault lines visible is essential to understanding the political nature of financial development.

Conclusion

This chapter has conceptualised financial development as a relational category, examining both the theoretical understandings and the economic practices that underpin it. In so doing, it has brought its political nature to the fore. Understanding financial development as a foremost social process draws attention to the external and internal relationships through which it is shaped and that it shapes in turn. On the one hand, this entails the relationship between financial change, autonomy and financialisation. On the other hand, it includes dynamics within the financial system, including the banking sector and capital markets. As I will discuss in more detail in Chapters 4 and 5, financial development has given rise to ongoing renegotiations of the relationship between financial and real economies, but also greater efforts to move beyond this dualism, most recently through efforts to promote social finance.

At the same time, however, financial development remains couched in a rather technical language, despite its political nature – as this chapter has demonstrated with regard to key concepts such as financial modernisation, financial deepening and financial inclusion. This framing of financial development as being foremost the purview of a depoliticised technocratic realm is problematic because it limits the contestability of finance through wider publics. And yet, as this chapter has shown, financial development is a process characterised by competing interests and values, the very definition of politics. In the next chapter, I examine in more detail the economic, political and social context of financial development in Malaysia. I will first trace the evolution of Malaysian capitalism through three distinct phases, before focusing on key actors and frameworks in financial policymaking.

Notes

1 For example, Johnson and Kwak (2010) examine rent-seeking behaviour of American banks before and during the 2008–2009 financial crisis. They show that rent-seeking was widespread and actually contributed to banks' risk-taking behaviour.

2   ASEAN is the Association of Southeast Asian Nations. It comprises Brunei Darussalam, Cambodia, Indonesia, Lao PDR, Malaysia, Myanmar, the Philippines, Singapore, Thailand and Viet Nam.

3   A detailed examination of this claim would go beyond the scope of this book. However, a couple of examples worth mentioning here are the role US banks played in the 1980s international debt crisis (Madrid 1992) or the 2013 'taper tantrum' triggered by the US Federal Reserve's announcement that it would taper its quantitative easing programme.

4   But see e.g. Rethel (2018) for an exploration of cultural shifts underpinning financialisation.

5   Bank Negara Malaysia, *Monthly Highlights and Statistics*, Series 3.5.12a.

6   This is a point that has been very eloquently made by Jomo and Lim in a recent Op-Ed (*The Edge Weekly*, 13 July 2019).

7   *New Straits Times* (27 February 2020).

8   *The Edge Financial Daily* (12 April 2017).

9   Bank Negara Malaysia Press Release (17 August 2018).

10 *New Straits Times* (16 August 2019).

11 For a full history, see CIMB (no date).

12 For the full data set and descriptor, please refer to the World Bank Global Financial Development Database (series GFDD.OI.01).

13 At the time, the term merchant banking was used. Since 2005, the term investment bank has been used, reflecting the consolidation of merchant banks, discount houses and stockbrokers (Azman *et al.* 2019).

3 The evolution of Malaysian capitalism and financial policymaking

With a population of 32 million people and a per capita GDP of around RM44,460, or US$11,415 according to World Bank data, Malaysia ranks as an upper middle-income country.[1] In the wider context of Asian development, Malaysia has moved ahead of its economically less powerful Southeast Asian counterparts, but not yet reached the status of the East Asian newly industrialised countries, namely Hong Kong, Taiwan, Singapore (another ASEAN member) and South Korea. Perhaps in Malaysia more so than elsewhere, financial policymaking is clearly and explicitly situated at the nexus of the two national goals of economic growth and redistribution.

As a consequence, since the 1970s, Malaysia looks back on a rich history of financial sector reform, with significant implications for how the banking system and the capital markets developed over subsequent decades. In comparison with other Asian capitalisms, the Malaysian financial system has been much more capital market-oriented, whilst at the same time maintaining a high level of state permeation. The next section will examine key characteristics and dynamics of Malaysian capitalism and their evolution over time. This will be followed by a section setting out the main actors in the financial policymaking process as well as the major legal and policy frameworks.

Malaysian capitalism in historical perspective

Since independence in 1957, Malaysian economic and financial policymaking has embraced both state-interventionist and market-liberal practices with significant implications for dynamics of ownership and control, a recurring theme in much of the Malaysian political economy literature (see e.g. Puthucheary 1960; Khor 1983; Gill 1985; Jesudason 1989; Jomo 1990; Bowie 1991; Gomez 1999; Gomez and Jomo 1999; Searle 1999; Gomez 2017).[2] While globalisation and the increasing integration of financial markets certainly are an important influence on Malaysian financial policymaking, as a former colony Malaya, and then Malaysia, started out with a financial system controlled by foreign – mainly British – banks. This only changed in the 1970s as a result of policy efforts to increase the indigenisation of the economy, including by strengthening the economic role of the Malays (Chantrasmi and Tham 1982).

In the just over six decades since independence the Malaysian economy has undergone significant transformations as this section will illustrate. From the current vantage point, two intersecting features stand out that make the Malaysian political economy rather distinctive. The first feature is one that is perhaps not commonly associated with a capitalist economy – although very common in capitalist Southeast Asia, and that is the extent of planning. Economic policymaking in Malaysia is orchestrated via various national-level and sectoral-level planning frameworks. Similarly, development objectives are spelled out in key economic initiatives and policy statements, including the New Economic Policy, Vision 2020 and, perhaps of more transitory nature, the New Economic Model, as I will discuss. The second key feature is the persistence of ethnic stratification that serves to legitimate both Malaysia's distinctive politics of patronage and, closely linked to this, the state-permeation of the economy. The remainder of this section will examine the impact of these features on the dynamics of Malaysian capitalism, following a loosely chronological order.

From independence to New Economic Policy

A colonial legacy and defining characteristic of the Malaysian political economy is that Malaysia is an ethnically diverse country. The most recent census puts the composition of the population at 91.8 per cent Malaysian citizens and 8.2 per cent non-citizens, with Malaysian citizens including 67.4 per cent Bumiputera (literally 'sons of the soil', a term often used to refer to ethnic Malays), 24.6 per cent Chinese and 7.3 per cent Indians (Department of Statistics 2011). Malaysia's multi-ethnic composition is also reflected in its party system (Crouch 1996). While Malaysia has been an electoral democracy since independence, Malaysian politics have been dominated by the United Malays National Organisation (UMNO) which represents the Malay majority. Between independence and the historic election of 2018, it led a coalition government, also comprising the Malaysian Chinese Association and the Malaysian Indian Congress, which respectively claim to represent the interests of Malaysia's Chinese and Indian communities. Since 1973, this coalition, also including a number of smaller parties, has been known as the *Barisan Nasional* (national front). However, not only was Malaysia's political system from the outset stratified along ethnic lines, there also existed an intimate relationship between ethnic group and type of occupation. While ethnic Malays were largely occupied in the rural economy and in the public service, the Chinese were concentrated in urban areas and involved in commercial activities.

In the first decade after independence, policymakers largely pursued a laissez-faire strategy that was characterised by a commitment to private enterprise, albeit in combination with selected developmental programmes targeted at Malays. Following the race riots of May 1969, the Malaysian government introduced what was widely perceived as an affirmative action programme to improve the economic status of ethnic Malays, or Bumiputeras. In 1971 it launched the New Economic Policy (NEP) whose two goals were to eradicate absolute poverty and to remove the identification of ethnicity with economic function (Government of Malaysia 1971). The government perceived redistribution, albeit coupled with the pursuit of economic growth, as fundamental to ensuring future social stability. The launch of the NEP foreshadowed a decade of heavier state intervention (Khor 1983; Jesudason 1989; Bowie 1991). Social engineering under the NEP took on various forms, including Malay quotas and privileges with regard to education, employment, shareholding and access to finance (Horii 1991). Moreover, ostensibly to promote Bumiputera economic interests, the state assumed an increasingly important economic role. While the NEP was implemented to address the stratification of society along ethnic lines, it actually reinforced the trend of an ethnically divided capitalism (Searle 1999). Both its identity as multi-ethnic polity and the NEP have given Malaysian capitalism its distinct form and also set it apart from other Asian capitalisms (Gomez 1999; Gomez and Jomo 1999; Searle 1999).

However, even in the early days of the NEP there existed different approaches towards its two goals within Malaysian policy circles (Faaland *et al.* 1990, 28–38). On the one hand, key agencies such as the Economic Planning Unit (EPU), the Treasury, Bank Negara Malaysia, the Statistics Department and the Federal Industrial Development Authority emphasised the economic growth aspect of the NEP. In so doing, they focused on economic modernisation and industrialisation. On the other hand, the Prime Minister's Department and the Department of National Unity pointed out socio-economic imbalances and favoured redistribution to reduce racial disparities. Thus, the NEP, ambiguously situated at the nexus of growth and distribution, was contested from the beginning. Indeed, the NEP's lack of specificity made it dependent on its interpretation by the government of the day (Case 2005).

For decades, the Malaysian government has used its control over capital and the banking system as a central means of economic policy-making (Bowie and Unger 1997, 71; Hamilton-Hart 2002, 101). The implementation of the NEP had important consequences for both the organisation and governance of the financial system. While the NEP was directed at the economy at large, certain of its aspects pertained specifically to the financial sector. The aim of the NEP was not only to increase Malay participation in the economy, but also to increase the share of the economy owned by Malays. Thus, an important element of the NEP was the restructuring of corporate ownership by means of financial restructuring along ethnic lines (Lim 1981; Gill 1985; Searle 1999). Therefore, the 1970s saw the preferential allocation of shares which were issued at discounted prices and that could only be purchased by Bumiputeras. In 1978, Malaysia's pre-eminent unit trust company, Permodalan Nasional Berhad (PNB) was created, institutionalising ethnically stratified shareholdership.[3] The expansion of the Malaysian equity market in the 1970s clearly was a by-product of the NEP.

However, the NEP also influenced the organisation of Malaysia's financial system in a wider sense, both by putting increased pressure on government finances and by conferring a crucial developmental role to the banking system. On the one hand, its implementation was expensive and associated with rising levels of government debt. The 1970s witnessed the rapid increase of development expenditure and a ballooning of the public sector. Fulfilling the goals of the NEP proved costly, in particular as the government had adopted a 'high-spending approach' which became manifested in the government's increased willingness to incur debt (Wong 1990, 110; see also Government of Malaysia 1976). Although total revenues were still higher than current expenditures, a gap opened when it came to development expenditure (Ismail 1982, 318). To cover the broadening deficit, Malaysia increased its borrowings abroad and began to issue more bonds domestically. To a large extent, the financial system became 'geared towards funding public sector development programmes' (Anwar 1995).

On the other hand, a crucial element of the NEP was the 'indigenisation' of the banking system, which had largely been controlled by foreign, namely British, interests at the time of independence and throughout the 1960s. This included the assumption of state control of a number of financial institutions, and a certain degree of government influence on bank lending (Lee and Jao 1982; Skully and Viksnins

1987, 141). Interest rates were set by the central bank, which basically precluded the market-determined allocation of capital. This is similar to what happened in other Asian developmental state models as discussed in the previous chapter (see also Amsden 1989; Wade 2004). Moreover in the mid-1970s, Bank Negara Malaysia introduced guidelines on lending, a move that coincided with a more development-oriented approach for banking (Government of Malaysia 1981, 256; Chantrasmi and Tham 1982; Zainal *et al.* 1996, 284). The target sectors were the Bumiputera community, small-scale businesses and industry, and agricultural enterprise (Government of Malaysia 1981, 305). However, the effectiveness of this policy has been questioned. The required percentage of loans allocated to priority sectors rapidly decreased from the original 50 per cent to 20 per cent and then to a periodically specified percentage of loans outstanding. From the late 1970s onwards, Bank Negara annually issued priority lending guidelines, which were kept relatively broad-based, and the interest rate regime was liberalised (Zainal *et al.* 1996, 284).

Mahathir's Vision 2020

During the first decade of the NEP the emphasis rested on redistribution, but under the premiership of Mahathir Mohamad (1981–2003) its growth orientation became more pronounced, with a focus on cultivating a Bumiputera Commercial and Industrial Community (Jomo 1990). The Mahathir years saw rapid economic growth, two major financial crises and a shift towards authoritarianism (Khoo 1995; Crouch 1996; Khoo 2003). While its identity as multi-ethnic state has been a core factor in the evolution of Malaysian capitalism, structural developments also have been of importance. Having already been negatively affected by the decline of international commodity prices and the deterioration of its terms of trade in the early 1980s, in 1985–1986 Malaysia suffered economic recession and financial crisis, resulting in a renewed focus on growth. One of the main pillars of this new focus was to concede a more significant role in the country's economic development to the private sector, for example through the privatisation of state assets (Government of Malaysia 1986; Khoo 1995; Jomo and Tan 2005). Along these lines, the position of private investment was strengthened. Moreover, since the mid-1980s, certain financial aspects of the NEP have been held 'in abeyance' and Malaysia has, selectively, implemented market-liberal reforms (Milne 1986; Jomo 1990). In particular, efforts were increased to attract foreign investment and the limits on foreign ownership were somewhat eased (Wong and Jomo 2005).

Malaysia's growth paradigm became enshrined further by Mahathir's articulation in 1991 of his *Vision 2020*, namely that Malaysia was to achieve developed country status by the year 2020, within three decades.[4] A core element of Vision 2020 was to create a prosperous society through the acceleration of GDP growth and 'the establishment of a *competitive* economy' (Mahathir 1991, 8, emphasis added). Shortly thereafter, the government published its *Privatisation Masterplan*, setting out the government's strategy, with a focus on infrastructure investment, privatisation of utilities and development of heavy industries conglomerates. The capital requirements were immense. The *Seventh Malaysia Plan* (1996–2000) envisaged a private investment requirement of RM350 billion. The World Bank projected private gross domestic fixed investment for the 1995–2004 period at over RM1.1 trillion for Malaysia to sustain its growth (World Bank 1995, ix). Much of this was to be raised in the capital market. Along with their expansion, there was a shift in the purpose of capital markets away from being an instrument of redistribution as in the equity restructurings during the first decade of the NEP, to being a facilitator, if not driver, of overall economic growth. Similarly, while planning remained an important aspect of policymaking, planning documents increasingly focused not only on detailing government expenditure, but also on setting private investment targets (Government of Malaysia 1991; 1996). In 1993, Khazanah Nasional Berhad, the investment arm of the Ministry of Finance, nowadays recognised as Malaysia's pre-eminent sovereign wealth fund, was incorporated (Lai 2012). In 1997, Khazanah began issuance of Shariah-compliant benchmark bonds, which was seen as an important step in the development of the corporate bond market (Bank Negara Malaysia 1999, 356–357).[5]

The same period, however, saw the increasingly influential role of money politics in Malaysia and a strengthening of the links between business and party organisations, often referred to as crony capitalism (Gomez and Jomo 1999).[6] Rent-seeking certainly was widespread in Malaysia before the Asian financial crisis of 1997–1998 (Gomez and Jomo 1999; Chin and Jomo 2000; Case 2005). Rents were not only granted to speed up Malaysia's industrialisation process (i.e. real economy) but also with regard to the restructuring of corporate equity (i.e. financial economy) under the NEP. Moreover, the effects of close ties between politics and business frequently spilled over into the financial sector. The rise of money politics, specifically with regard to party elections, and closely related, the equity and property bubbles of the early 1990s overshadowed the relationship between financial economy and real economy (Gomez and Jomo 1999). Furthermore, Malaysia continued to liberalise its capital account to attract portfolio invest-ment, with the ambition to establish itself as a regional, and to some extent even international, financial centre (Athukorala 2001).

The early 1990s witnessed significant portfolio capital inflows. Attempts to slow these down were undermined by political interest in keeping the overheating stock market going (Tan 2003; Ariff and Khalid 2005). The onset of the Asian crisis brought on a rapid reversal of capital flows, resulting in the rapid depreciation of the ringgit and a plunging stock market. However, Malaysia did not have to seek IMF assistance, mainly because of relatively low foreign debt levels, at least in regional comparison, and the ability of local institutions – the EPF and Petronas – to step in as investors-of-last-resort (Abdelal and Alfaro 2003; Tan 2003). Nevertheless, Malaysia's initial response was a 'self-initiated adjustment programme' to regain investor confidence (Bank Negara Malaysia 1998, 99). As the economic situation deteriorated, so did the political one, ultimately resulting in the fallout between Mahathir and his deputy and finance minister Anwar Ibrahim over increasingly divergent approaches to economic policy (Haggard 2000).

The imposition of capital controls in September 1998 certainly went against the orthodoxy of the time (Haggard 2000; Islam and Chowdhury 2000; Nesadurai 2000). Nonetheless, in the wake of the crisis, Malaysia implemented a series of market-supporting reforms and undertook new efforts to cultivate international investors. Thus, perhaps paradoxic-ally, the 1997–1998 financial crisis and Malaysia's at the time idiosyn-cratic policy response did not, as it is often assumed, put a brake on the increasing importance of financial markets, financial motives, finan-cial institutions and financial elites in the operation of the Malaysian economy and its governing institutions, to lightly paraphrase Epstein (2019, 380; see also 2005). Instead, it actually reinforced these dynamics, a trend that was to continue under Mahathir's successors.

Najib's New Economic Model

Mahathir held his office until 2003 when he resigned to hand over to his successor, Abdullah Ahmad Badawi. The government of Abdullah Badawi (2003–2009) has been widely credited with the country's tenta-tive political opening post-Mahathir (Welsh and Chin 2013). In 2004, it launched the 'GLC transformation programme' aimed at enhancing efficiency and combined with a shift towards neoliberal management practices such as key performance indicators (Putrajaya Committee 2006). Along these lines, and following the appointment of Azman Mokthar as its CEO, Khazanah underwent a transformation from being a rather passive trustee of what it used to term 'non-financial public enterprises' to increasingly activist investor, in Malaysia and abroad. The aim of creating shareholder value was added to its nation-building agenda. Khazanah also became a significant presence in the country's domestic as well as the nascent regional bond and *sukuk* markets. Moreover, not only did Khazanah drive the adoption of KPIs in its portfolio companies, but it also encouraged the greater use of sukuk in their financing.[7]

Following the loss of Barisan Nasional's two-thirds majority in the 2008 general election, Najib Razak succeeded Abdullah as prime minister in April 2009. Upon coming into office, Najib (2009–2018) initiated a series of reform programmes, most prominently the Government Transformation Programme and the Economic Transformation Programme. In their support, he created a new planning agency, Pemandu (Performance Management and Delivery Unit). Staffed with corporate executives, Pemandu was established with the aim of bringing market expertise into the government apparatus, thus contributing to the dual transformation of both economy and government. Working closely with strategic management consultancies such as McKinsey, Pemandu was the author of the government's ambitious Economic and Government Transformation roadmaps. However, Pemandu repeatedly came under criticism from both the opposition as well as pro-Malay groups such as Perkasa.[8]

In 2010, Najib launched the New Economic Model, aimed at reducing state intervention and doubling per capita income between 2010 and 2020. It was framed as a replacement of the NEP, with a focus on 'race-based affirmative action' (Khoo 2018, 246). Following the loss of the popular vote in the 2013 general election, the Najib government, retaining a parliamentary majority, shifted to more redistributive policymaking, once more along ethnic lines. To this end, it launched its Bumiputera Economic Empowerment Programme.[9] More generally, under Najib, tensions between the shift towards performance-oriented marketisation (of both economy and polity) and entrenched clientelism as a dominant governance strategy in Malaysia's ethnically stratified capitalism broke very visibly to the fore. The contestation of Pemandu was a case in point.

Under Abdullah and then Najib, the role of the Ministry of Finance as a shareholder in the Malaysian economy became increasingly pervasive (Gomez 2017). Whilst government ownership is nothing new in Malaysia, the nature and quality of state-permeation has changed over time, bringing Malaysia closer to what Wang (2015) has termed the 'shareholding state'. This becomes clear, for example, when we look at the extent and mode of state-ownership in the financial sector. In the early post-independence period, foreign-owned financial institutions dominated the Malaysian political economy (Gill 1985, 8). Following the implementation of the NEP from the early 1970s onwards, the share of locally owned financial institutions increased significantly. In subsequent decades, the state became a more and more important shareholder. But it was only in the wake of the Asian crisis that this coincided with an increasingly financialised approach to economic management. The shareholding state thus also became an increasingly important means of political stability. Closely related, the post-Mahathir period also saw a consolidation of the shift within Malaysia's distinctive model of ethnically stratified state capitalism from close political-business ties to ever closer government-business ties.

In the context of the struggle between interventionist and liberal economic forces, Malaysia's uneasy political settlement was undermined by a system of what Khoo (2018, 247) has called 'unchecked corruption', of which the 1MDB scandal became the focal point. Malaysia's second sovereign wealth fund, 1MDB, had been created in 2009 as the Terengganu Investment Authority. Upon coming into office, Najib brought it under control of the Ministry of Finance and, in his role as first finance minister, served as its advisory board chairman. In the years that followed, 1MDB went on a borrowing spree, which famously included the issuance of a series of bonds in 2012 and 2013 that were underwritten and arranged by the Singapore office of US investment bank Goldman Sachs. The 1MDB saga is thus also a cautionary tale about the entanglements of global finance (see also Hamilton-Hart 2016).

Nevertheless, in terms of domestic financial stability, the impact of the 1MDB scandal was buffered by Malaysia's distinctive, state-capitalist configuration. This was despite the reputational damage, outflow of foreign funds, and, how the incoming Pakatan Harapan government found out to its dismay, deteriorating budget situation. In 2015, Malaysian GLICs were called upon to sell overseas assets and repatriate the proceeds to stabilise the domestic economy.[10] Incidentally, this allowed EPF and KWAP to cash out on some of their London property investments just before the Brexit referendum.[11] Indeed, Malaysian institutions have a track record of stepping in as investors-of-last resort at times of crisis. Examples include EPF and Petronas acting as investors-of-last resort during the 1997–1998 Asian crisis, EPF's RM5 billion loan to ValueCap during the 2008 global crisis, and again the support provided by domestic institutional investors during the 2020 COVID-19 pandemic.[12]

Following the fallout from the 1MDB scandal, Barisan Nasional lost its parliamentary majority in the 2018 general election. The opposition coalition, Pakatan Harapan had campaigned on a promise to not appoint politicians to corporate leadership roles. Upon coming into office, it undertook a major executive management reshuffle, bringing in a new slate of corporate executives and key bureaucrats (Chin 2018). However, its coalition fell apart in February 2020, culminating in the resignation of Mahathir Mohamad. His *Perikatan Nasional* successor, Muhyiddin Yassin swiftly reverted to making an extensive range of political appointments. Nevertheless, this is the environment that financial policymakers must navigate and that has shaped the trajectories of financial development.

Financial policymaking: key actors and major frameworks

The NEP has proved an enduring influence on the organisation of the Malaysian financial system (e.g. Singh 1984; Hamilton-Hart 2002; Wong *et al.* 2005; Ang 2008; Cook 2008). Likewise, its statist approach continues to have a particularly powerful hold over the imagination of both policymakers and society, whilst Malaysian capitalism remains shrouded in the veils of crony capitalism and ethnicity. Nevertheless, somewhat unremarked there has been another trend and that has been the greater financialisation of Malaysian capitalism, specifically the increasing importance of finance (not 'just' money) in the 'operation of the economy *and its governing institutions*' to borrow once more Epstein's (2019, 380; my emphasis) phrase. To further elucidate this point, I now turn to the dynamics of financial policymaking in Malaysia.

Malaysia's integration with global markets makes the distinctive character of its political economy the more remarkable, given that integration is usually associated with a higher degree of international harmonisation (Elkins and Simmons 2004). However, regarding the financial sector, Malaysia's experience has been mixed. A period of openness in the 1950s and 1960s characterised by the dominance of foreign banks, was followed by increased closure in the 1970s and the early 1980s as the economy underwent economic restructuring along ethnic lines. This, in turn, led to a decade of relative openness and the liberalisation of the capital account, only to result in the Asian crisis of 1997–1998. In its wake, Malaysia embraced a catalogue of financial sector reforms, including the consolidation of the banking system and the development of capital markets to further its financial development agenda. Before examining these developments in more detail in Chapters 4 and 5, in the remainder of this chapter, I will present a brief overview of the main actors and frameworks of the financial policymaking process. The following two chapters will then provide a fine-grained analysis of the politics of financial development in Malaysia focusing on the banking system and capital markets, respectively.

Ministry of Finance and the government-linked investment companies (GLICs)

Since independence, the Ministry of Finance has played a significant role in Malaysia's economic development. Indeed, for most of its history, the Ministry of Finance shared this economic policymaking role with the Economic Planning Unit in the Prime Minister's Office, created in 1961 to take over the planning function from the Treasury (Ismail 1982, 336). Following the fallout from the Asian crisis and the arrest of Anwar Ibrahim, Mahathir took on the position of First Finance Minister, merging the portfolios of finance minister and prime minister to some extent. Whilst the Ministry of Finance remained operational, and indeed the position of Second Finance Minister was created to oversee its everyday affairs, it was thus brought under much more direct political control. This system would continue throughout the premierships of both Abdullah Badawi and Najib Razak, and only go on to change with the appointment of Lim Guan Eng as Finance Minister under the short-lived Pakatan Harapan government. Since then, and in a significant departure from prior practice, the position has been held by Zafrul Aziz, a former banker with no political affiliation. Table 3.1 provides a list of Finance Ministers in chronological order of appointment.

In addition to its treasury and economic policy functions, the Ministry of Finance also has oversight, and in a number of cases even control, of a dense network of government-linked companies (GLCs). Moreover, in Malaysia, as already hinted at, there exist significant pools of domestic capital, managed by state institutions – so-called government-linked investment companies (GLICs). An important role in this regard is played by the Ministry's subsidiary Ministry of Finance Incorporated (or MoF Inc.). Gomez (2017, 19–27) provides a detailed account of its trajectory, tracing it from its establishment by the 1957 Ministry of Finance (Incorporated) Act all the way through to the Najib administration, by which time it had accumulated an 'interest' in more than a hundred companies. Importantly, this included the two GLICs PNB and Khazanah as discussed in the previous section in the context of the NEP and Vision 2020, respectively. Both PNB and Khazanah have played vital roles in the development of the financial system as I will explore in the next two chapters. Nevertheless, just looking at their

Table 3.1 Ministers of Finance

First Minister	In Office	Second Minister	In Office
Hau-Shaik Lee	1957–1959		
Tan Siew Sin	1959–1969		
	1970–1974		
Abdul Razak	1969–1970		
Hussein Onn	1974–1976		
Razaleigh Hamzah	1976–1984		
Daim Zainuddin	1985–1991		
Anwar Ibrahim	1991–1998		
Mahathir Mohamad	1998–1999	Mustapa Mohamed	1998–1999
Daim Zainuddin	1999–2001		
Mahathir Mohamad	2001–2003	Jamaluddin Jarjis	2002–2004
Abdullah Badawi	2003–2008	Nor Mohamed Yakcop	2004–2009
Najib Razak	2008*–2018	Ahmad Husni Hanadzlah	2009–2016
		Johari Abdul Ghani	2016–2018
Lim Guan Eng	2018–2020		
Zafrul Aziz	2020–		

Source: Ministry of Finance website; information on second ministers compiled from *The Star* (15 January 2004); *The Edge* (28 June 2016); *The Star* (17 September 2018)
Note: *Ministry of Finance website states 2009

financial weight gives an idea of their importance. By the end of 2019, PNB's assets-under-management had reached RM312 billion, whilst Khazanah had reached a net asset value of RM73.1 billion.[13]

In terms of the size of their investment portfolios, of even greater significance are the pension fund GLICs. These include the EPF, Malaysia's mandatory pension savings scheme for private sector workers, established in 1951, with total assets at the end of 2019 standing at RM924.75 billion, by far the largest institutional investor in Malaysia.[14] Second, there is the Retirement Fund (Incorporated) (Kumpulan Wang Persaraan (Diperbadankan) or KWAP), the pension scheme for public sector workers, with assets-under-management of RM140.8 billion at the end of 2017.[15] Third, there is the Armed Forces Fund Board (Lembaga Tabung Angkatan Tentera or LTAT) – established in 1972 and under the oversight of the Ministry of Defence, with assets-under-management of RM9.48 billion at the end of 2019.[16] Finally, not a pension fund, but also intended to facilitate long-term saving is the Pilgrims Fund Board (Lembaga Tabung Haji or LTH), established in the 1960s as a vehicle to allow Malaysia's Muslim, and at that time very much rural, population to save for the pilgrimage. As of end of December 2018, its assets stood at RM76.5 billion.[17]

Together, assets managed by these six GLICs amounted to more than RM1.5 trillion in 2019, much of which was domestically invested. By comparison, the market capitalisation of the stock market, Bursa Malaysia, stood at RM1.04 trillion, whilst bonds and sukuk outstanding came to a total of RM1.34 trillion, of which 57 per cent had been issued by the government, as of end 2019.[18] Moreover, through its GLICs, the state also emerges as a significant shareholder in the banks, including the country's three biggest banks, Maybank, CIMB and Public Bank as I will discuss in more detail in the next chapter. However, this system has not been without its criticisms. For example, Thomas Pepinsky (2012, 247) argues that '[t]hrough such institutions, economic policies – created with an eye toward improving the economic status of Malays – still reward political efficacy rather than economic efficiency'. The impact of the GLICs is also highlighted in studies published by, the Institute for Democracy and Economic Affairs (IDEAS), an advocate of reducing the government's role in the corporate sector (e.g. Lau and Nur Zulaikha 2020).

The regulators – Bank Negara Malaysia and the Securities Commission

At the time of the Asian crisis, both Bank Negara and the Securities Commission were under the oversight of the Ministry of Finance. In its aftermath both BNM and the Securities Commission were put on a stronger footing through post-AFC legislation. Nevertheless, as discussed in the previous chapter, statutory independence does not necessarily result in greater *de facto* autonomy in a context where regulatory personnel are subservient to the government of the day. Correspondingly, even at a time where autonomy is narrowly circumscribed, bureaucracies can have capacity to formulate and implement their own policies, drawing on technocratic expertise and moral leadership (see also Hamilton-Hart 2002, 118).

In this regard, the NEP also had important implications for the management and governance of the financial system. During the first decade of *laissez-faire* economic policymaking, the task of regulating the financial system was shared between the treasury and the central bank, Bank Negara Malaysia, which had been established in 1959. Although organisationally subordinated to the Ministry of Finance, since its inception BNM had been an influential institution led by strong, well respected personalities which had instilled it with scope for autonomy (Singh 1984). However, Hamilton-Hart (2002, 118) notes that from the mid-1980s onwards, Bank Negara increasingly came under informal political

Table 3.2 Bank Negara Malaysia governors

Governor	Time in Office
W.H. Wilcock	1959–1962
Ismail Mohamed Ali	1962–1980
Abdul Aziz Taha	1980–1985
Jaffar Hussein	1985–1994
Ahmad Mohd Don	1994–1998
Ali Abul Hassan Sulaiman	1998–2000
Dr. Zeti Akhtar Aziz	2000–2016
Muhammad Ibrahim	2016–2018
Nor Shamsiah Mohd Yunus	2018–

Source: Bank Negara Malaysia website

pressure. Table 3.2 provides a list of Bank Negara governors in chronological order of appointment.

In June 1985, Jaffar Hussein, a former commercial banker, came to head BNM, a move in line with the government's increasing private sector orientation. However, disagreements between the former governor, Abdul Aziz and Mahathir's newly appointed Finance Minister, the influential businessman Daim Zainuddin, are also thought to have played a role in the new appointment (Hamilton-Hart 2002, 118). His successor, Ahmad Mohd Don, similarly had been a career banker before becoming governor of BNM in 1994. His resignation during the Asian crisis, following disagreement about the implementation of capital controls, heralded the return of career bureaucrats heading the central bank. After a short interlude with Ali Abul Hassan, previously the Director General of the Economic Planning Unit, at the helm, Dr Zeti, who had already been acting governor during the crisis, became the first woman governor. Her tenure saw significant changes in the financial system, including the consolidation of the banking system and the shift towards Islamic finance as I will discuss in the next chapter.

Since its inception, Bank Negara has derived significant moral authority from the standing of its governors.[19] Moreover, it played a central role in the evolution of the Malaysian political economy. However, the relationship between Bank Negara and the government of the day was not always straightforward, resulting in tensions between its technocratic expertise and political loyalties. At the same time, there has been limited scope for pushback. This became perhaps most visible during the Najib era. Fault lines appeared both with regard to the central bank's investigation into the 1MDB scandal and the question of who was to succeed Dr Zeti, whose term came to an end in April 2016. The short tenure of her successor, Muhammad Ibrahim, saw the departure of two deputy governors from the Bank. Moreover, it was overshadowed by a land deal entered between Bank Negara and the federal government in January 2018 that was dubbed by a weekly newspaper as 'the most controversial property deal of the year'.[20] Subsequent to the change in government, former deputy governor Nor Shamsiah returned to the Bank to become its next governor.

However, not only did Bank Negara lead on a number of financial system reforms in the first decade after the Asian crisis, at times in a somewhat uneasy relationship with the Ministry of Finance. It was itself subject to reform, of which the legislation of monetary policy autonomy, enhanced financial supervisory capacity and strengthening of its Shariah Advisory Council are perhaps the most noteworthy. Along these lines, its regulatory capacity also increased with regard to both the training and number of staff. Between 1997 and 2019, staffing levels at Bank Negara nearly doubled (see also Table 3.3).[21]

Bank Negara has historically played an active role in regional and international regulatory networks (Singh 1984). It was one of the drivers behind the establishment of a Southeast Asian voting group to represent the interests of Southeast Asian economies at the IMF, World Bank and ADB. It also played an instrumental role in the creation of the South East Asian Central Banks Research and Training Centre (SEACEN), which was established as a legal entity in Kuala Lumpur in 1982. Furthermore, Bank Negara has also played a leading role in the setting up of a number of global governance organisations for Islamic finance. This includes the Islamic Financial Services Board, which was established in Kuala Lumpur in 2002, and the International Islamic Liquidity Management Corporation, created in 2010. In addition to setting up formal institutions, Bank Negara also regularly hosts

Table 3.3 Bank Negara Malaysia staff levels

Year	Number
1997	1,595
2000	1,876
2005	2,345
2010	2,734
2015	2,935
2019	3,114

Source: Bank Negara Malaysia (various years) *Annual Report*

fact finding missions and provides capacity building programmes for regulators from around the world, including on topics such as Islamic finance and financial inclusion. In so doing, Bank Negara has built a significant track record of pursuing networked approaches to regional and international governance and *de facto* become an influential arbiter of what is deemed financial best practice in the Global South.

With regard to the regulation of the capital market, Bank Negara was assisted in its efforts to develop Malaysia's financial system by another body, the Capital Issues Committee (CIC). Having been set up in 1968 to help regulate the market with 'moral suasion', the CIC became a legal body with the 1983 Securities Industry Act. It was foremost a safeguard mechanism or 'watchdog committee', set up to control the pricing and timing of new securities and thus to ensure the orderly development of the market (Singh 1984, 198). However, as Jomo and Gomez (2000, 289) highlight, in the 1970s with the implementation of the NEP it gained increasing importance with the promotion of Malay stock ownership. Moreover, while playing a more discretionary role in the beginning, over the years it assumed an increasingly formal role. The 1983 Securities Industry Act detailed its authority and functions. It began to publish guidelines for the new issuance of securities. The number of staff members within the CIC secretariat increased steadily throughout the 1980s.

The CIC was closely associated with Bank Negara, which housed its secretariat and provided a higher-ranking Bank Negara official as its secretary general. Furthermore, it was chaired by Bank Negara's governor (Singh 1984, 3). The committee also consisted of representatives from other agencies and the private sector. Its inaugural meeting was attended by representatives from the Ministry of Finance, the Ministry of Commerce and Industry, the Registrar of Companies and the private sector (Securities Commission 2004, 42). The CIC met periodically. It assessed whether a new security was in line with policies, in particular whether the proceedings of a bond issuance were invested in suitable sectors. In a 'use of funds' approach, monetary policy considerations frequently were decisive in whether an issue was approved. However, under Daim, the CIC was removed from BNM's control, and placed under the purview of the Ministry of Finance, incidentally the first step towards setting up a separate entity in charge of regulating the capital market (Hamilton-Hart 2002, 118; SC 2004). In 1993, the Securities Commission was founded as the main regulator for the Malaysian capital market; it resumed operations in 1994.

With the establishment of the Securities Commission, Malaysia shifted towards a twin-peak regulatory system. In the following decade,

Table 3.4 Securities Commission chairmen

Chairman	Time in Office
Mohd Munir Abdul Majid	1993–1999
Ali Abdul Kadir	1999–2004
Md Nor Md Yusof	2004–2006
Zarinah Anwar	2006–2012
Ranjit Ajit Singh	2012–2018
Syed Zaid Albar	2018–

Source: Securities Commission (various years) *Annual Report*

the SC successively assumed greater responsibilities. In 2000, it became the single authority in charge of corporate bond issuance. From the outset, the SC adopted an activist developmental stance, which is especially visible with regard to the development of the Islamic capital market. Along these lines, an Islamic Instruments Group was established in 1994, out of which the Shariah Advisory Council of the Securities Commission should evolve. As in the case of Bank Negara, the Securities Commission also derives autonomy from the standing of its chairmen. Table 3.4 provides a list of Securities Commission chairmen, in chronological order of appointment. In this context, it is worth mentioning that in terms of their professional backgrounds, the SC tends to appoint market practitioners as relative outsiders as opposed to both the party officials that have traditionally helmed the Ministry of Finance and the career technocrats that have dominated the rota of governors at BNM.

Legal and policy frameworks

Malaysia's twin-peak regulatory system is governed by separate legal frameworks. Thus, the role of the two main financial regulators in Malaysia – Bank Negara Malaysia and Securities Commission Malaysia – are set out in the *Central Bank of Malaysia Act (2009)* and the *Securities Commission Malaysia Act (1993)*, including several Amendments that were enacted over the years. With the reallocation of responsibilities to the SC, it was important to clarify its working relationship with BNM and MoUs were signed to this end in 2002, 2007 and 2012. Moreover, on a practical level, BNM and the SC cooperate for example in joint working groups.

In the wake of the mid-1980s economic crisis, the government had introduced the *Banking and Financial Institutions Act (BAFIA) 1989*, providing a framework for the 'integrated supervision' of the Malaysian financial system and strengthening the supervisory powers of BNM (Bank Negara Malaysia 1999, 100). In 2013, it was repealed and replaced by the *Financial Services Act (FSA) 2013*, which also served to consolidate a number of other, previously separate, legislations. One of the major changes in the FSA is that it recognises the concept of financial holding companies (FHCs) and gives Bank Negara the power to regulate them (Tan and Lee 2013). The FSA also strengthens consumer protection, for example prohibiting financial institutions from exerting 'undue pressure' on their customers (Ghazali and Kandiah 2014, 6).

The legal framework for Islamic banks was also overhauled and the government repealed the *Islamic Banking Act 1983* and replaced it with the *Islamic Financial Services Act (IFSA) 2013*. IFSA 2013 considerably strengthens the Shariah supervision of Islamic financial institutions both in processual terms and with regard to enforcement. It grants Bank Negara Malaysia the power to 'specify standards on Shariah matters … in accordance with the advice or ruling of the Shariah Advisory Council' (section 29). Islamic financial institutions, their senior management and Shariah committee members are legally obliged to comply with the standards specified by Bank Negara. Failure to comply incurs imprisonment of no more than eight years or a fine of no more than RM25 million or both. Furthermore, IFSA mandates Islamic financial institutions to conduct Shariah audits.

Capital markets are governed by the *Capital Markets and Services Act (CMSA) 2007*, which consolidates the *Securities Industry Act 1983* and the *Futures Industry Act 1993*, 'to regulate and to provide for matters relating to the activities, markets and intermediaries in the capital markets'. The role of the Shariah Advisory Council of the SC in the governance of Islamic capital markets is firmly enshrined by the 2010 Amendment of the CMSA. According to the amendment, in case of different interpretations, its rulings 'prevail' over the rulings of firm-level registered Shariah advisors. This entrenches further its authority in the Shariah governance of Islamic capital markets in Malaysia. Moreover, they are binding not only over Islamic financial firms, but also over courts and arbitrators.

Malaysia has a long tradition of economic development planning (Faaland *et al.* 1990). The first five-year *Malaysia Plan*, aimed at tackling the country's economic and social issues, dates back to the mid-1960s. The role of planning was ratcheted up with the implementation of the NEP. In 1971, the first *Outline Perspective Plan* was released, entailing a much longer planning horizon of 20 years. These national-level planning frameworks have been complemented by sectoral plans, such as the 1991 *Privatisation Masterplan* mentioned earlier. Juanita Elias (2020) highlights the importance of these plans as 'frames of reference' for both policy and market – and even civil society – actors. Along these lines, the publication of analogous plans for the financial sector can be traced back to the aftermath of the Asian financial crisis of 1997–1998.

Recognising the lingering effect of the crisis on domestic financial activity and Malaysia's international competitiveness, Bank Negara and the Securities Commission moved to drafting ten-year development plans. Both the *Financial Sector Master Plan* (FSMP) and the *Capital Market Masterplan* (CMP) were released in 2001. The plans set out each regulator's vision for the markets under their jurisdiction as well as a number of objectives and more detailed recommendations to be achieved during the planning period. In 2011, *Capital Market Masterplan 2* (CMP2) and the *Financial Sector Blueprint* (FSBP) were published, setting the framework for the subsequent decade. Aaron Pitluck (2013) highlights the importance of these planning exercises not just in terms of coordinating the financial bureaucracy, but also in providing certainty to investors. In so doing, the plans have become a distinct means of communication of the regulators with both domestic and international financial communities, which are also engaged through extended consultations in preparation of these plans.

Financial development planning is broadly nested within the wider planning framework. Thus, for instance, CMP2 situates its agenda of 'growth with governance' within the discourse of the New Economic Model (Securities Commission 2011). Moreover, the Plans also indicate where the regulators see scope for legal reforms, take for example the recommendation to review CMSA 'to widen the range of asset classes for intermediation' in CMP2. Likewise, FSBP recommended the enactment of a new consumer credit law. However, not all these recommendations have translated into change; a case in point is the merger of the Shariah Advisory Councils of Bank Negara and the Securities Commission recommended in CMP, a reform that did not happen.[22]

In addition to these major planning frameworks, the Malaysian financial authorities also pursue more topical initiatives. These include the *Strategy Paper on Value-based Intermediation* released by Bank Negara in 2017 (discussed in Chapter 4) and the *Sustainable and Responsible Investment Roadmap for the Malaysian Capital Market* published by the Securities Commission in 2019 (discussed in Chapter 5). Likewise, Malaysian regulators have contributed to international and regional initiatives and frameworks, in particular in areas where they see complementarities with Malaysian developmental ambitions (see e.g. IOSCO 2004; ASEAN Capital Markets Forum 2017).

Conclusion

Economic policymaking in Malaysia has a history of espousing both state-interventionist and market-liberal elements. A distinctive characteristic is the special status of Bumiputeras, i.e. ethnic Malays, both as authors and targets of policy interventions. Constituting a political majority, the economic marginalisation of Bumiputeras, especially in the first decades after independence, has served as an important justification for distributive policymaking ever since. At the same time, the form that this support has taken has changed considerably, in particular in the context of the privatisation and industrialisation drives of the 1980s and early 1990s. The intensification of state-sponsored financialisation in the wake of the Asian crisis has also had an impact as I will discuss in the next two chapters.

In terms of financial development, the effects of policy frameworks such as the NEP, Vision 2020 and the New Economic Model have been ambiguous. Initially favouring the banking system, from the late 1980s the shift towards capital markets became more pronounced. Taken together, Malaysia's historical development and the distinctive way in which financial policymaking has become institutionalised have contributed significantly to the shape of Malaysian capitalism and its evolution, both in form and substance. The next two chapters will dive deeper into the politics of financial development, focusing on changes in the banking system and capital markets.

Notes

1 World Bank (Series SP.POP.TOTL; NY.GDP.PCAP.KN; NY.GDP.PCAP. CD). See Appendix B for more details.
2 By necessity, this overview of the evolution of Malaysian capitalism is very broad-brushed and focused on the development of the financial system. However, there exists a long tradition of excellent political economy scholarship in and on Malaysia. I very much encourage readers to delve into this scholarship to develop a much richer understanding than I am able to convey in a few short pages. This includes the early postcolonial political economy scholarship of James J. Puthucheary and Syed Hussein Alatas, work by Martin Khor Kok Peng and Jomo Kwame Sundaram, and the forensic analyses of E. Terence Gomez. Indeed, in this book I highlight some of the ways in which shifts in the 'ownership and control of corporate

Malaysia' that Gomez (2017) diagnoses intersect with and reinforce socially suboptimal financialisation dynamics.

3 Unit trusts are collective investment schemes similar to mutual funds.

4 Strictly speaking, the NEP was intended to only last until 1990, and was followed by the National Development Policy (1990–2000) and the National Vision Policy (2001–2010). However, these policy frameworks never fully managed to replace the NEP.

5 At the time, the instrument was called a 'Murabahah bond'; nowadays these sorts of financial instruments would be referred to as sukuk rather than bonds.

6 Interestingly, this was initially alleged by Japanese observers (*The Economist*, 24 June 1995).

7 As a sovereign wealth fund, Khazanah does not declare any dividends to the public. However, it pays a dividend to the government which amounted to RM1 billion in 2019 (*The Edge*, 2 March 2020). Pundits have detected in this a shift towards a bigger role for institutional investors in generating state revenue (*The Edge*, 7 October 2019).

8 *The Malaysian Insider* (28 December 2010).

9 *The Star* (14 September 2013).

10 *The Edge Financial Daily* (25 November 2015).

11 *The Star* (25 January 2017).

12 *The Star* (22 October 2008); *MalayMail* (14 March 2020).

13 *The Star* (4 May 2020); *The Edge* (2 March 2020). Under the Pakatan Harapan government, oversight of PNB and Khazanah moved to the Prime Minister's Department.

14 *The Edge* (2 February 2020).

15 *Malaysian Reserve* (13 May 2019).

16 *MalayMail* (18 May 2020).

17 *Malaysian Reserve* (28 January 2020). As of January 2019, the Pakatan Harapan government put Tabung Haji under the supervision of Bank Negara.

18 *The Star* (31 December 2019); *Bond and Sukuk Information Exchange* (18 March 2020).

19 *The Star* (8 August 2009).

20 *The Edge* (8 January 2019).

21 Bank Negara staffing levels had declined significantly by the time of the Asian crisis to 1,595 in 1997 and 1,560 in 1998, having previously reached a high of 2,865 staff in 1995 (Hamilton-Hart 2002, appendix 5).

22 However, FSBP also recommends 'Establishing a single legislated body as the apex authority on Shariah matters for institutions offering Islamic financial services in Malaysia' (Bank Negara Malaysia 2011, 113).

4   Financial modernisation and banking reform

The Asian financial crisis of 1997–1998 paved the way for financial sector reform in Malaysia. The previous chapter discussed changes in financial regulation, including the legal autonomy of the central bank, Bank Negara, the strengthening of its financial supervisory capacity and the further entrenchment of the shift to a twin-peak regulatory model. However, the Asian crisis also brought about change at the market level. It set the stage for a series of state-led consolidations in the banking sector, both deepening and broadening the market.

First, following a wave of state mandated mergers, the number of local banking institutions was reduced by more than half. Second, with the demise of finance companies, the shift to a universal banking model was further consolidated. Third, Islamic finance became increasingly ubiquitous, given both the growing number of Islamic banks and the growing share of Islamic finance in the banking system. Nevertheless, the impact on the banking sector was far from straightforward. In the aftermath of the bank consolidations, bank concentration rose substantially until it peaked in 2009. There was also a sustained shift from lending for productive capacity, including manufacturing, to consumer finance – credit cards, car loans and residential property – highlighting questions about the social purpose of finance. At the same time, the regional orientation of Malaysia's big banks also increased.

This chapter is divided into three parts. The next section will discuss financial reforms in the banking sector. The section thereafter will examine some of the implications of these changes, with an emphasis on financialisation dynamics. The third section will then shift the focus a little bit and highlight regulatory efforts to nurture so-called 'value-based intermediation'. In this chapter, I focus on changes in the banking system. I will discuss closely related efforts to expand the role of capital markets in the next chapter.

Consolidating the banking sector

Since the late 1980s, and especially so against the background of the Uruguay Round of trade negotiations of the early 1990s, Bank Negara had been keen to strengthen the competitiveness of the domestic banking sector. In 1994, it introduced a two-tiered approach to bank regulation, to encourage the merger of smaller banks with bigger multi-purpose banks (Chin 2005, 125). However, with the heating up of the stock market, there was little market pressure for bank consolidation. In the aftermath of the Asian crisis, Bank Negara pushed more force-fully for local bank consolidation, starting with the finance companies in January 1998. In July 1999, it announced that the country's existing 21 banks were to be submerged within six anchor banks. Cook (2008, 87–93) details significant discontent with these bank merger plans. Ultimately, the backlash resulted in the announcement of a new merger plan in October 1999 that allowed for ten anchor banks (see also Chin 2005, 129). Table 4.1 illustrates changes in the number and types of financial institutions, including both local and foreign banks. It clearly demonstrates a significant transformation, including the reduction of the overall numbers of financial institutions. Moreover, the bank con-solidation plan clearly signalled the power of the ethnically stratified state over the financial sector. As Terence Gomez (2013, 67) succinctly summarises,

> There appears to be a link between the consolidation of the finan-cial sector and the subsequent fall in domestic investment in the economy. Through the consolidation exercise, the government instantaneously removed ownership and control of banks by owners who had long held a major presence in the sector. This was an indication of the might of a strong state, and a clear sign to pri-vate investors of their limited capacity to protect their corporate assets. Financial capital was now firmly embedded in the hands of the state or well-connected business people.

Nevertheless, building on the discussion in Chapter 2 on the ambigu-ities of measuring financial development, bank classifications have also changed over time. Most notable is the demise of the finance companies, following the wave of mergers of the late 1990s and early 2000s, with each other and with commercial banks. Moreover, whilst the number of commercial banks has decreased from 35 in 1998 to 26 in 2020, the number of Islamic banks has increased from 1 to 16. However, the

Table 4.1 Number and type of banking institutions

	1998	2000	2005	2010	2015	2020
Commercial Banks	10 (tier 1) 25 (tier 2)	32	23	23	27	26
Finance Companies	4 (tier 1) 27 (tier 2)	20	4	–	–	–
Merchant/Investment Banks	6 (tier 1) 6 (tier 2)	12	10	15	11	11
Islamic Banks	1 (tier 2)	2	6	17	16	16

Source: BNM, *Monthly Highlights and Statistics* (Series 5.1)

majority of these were created as subsidiaries, backed by either domestic or foreign banks. Indeed, following the granting of a banking licence to MBSB Bank in 2018, there are now three stand-alone, full-fledged domestic Islamic banks in Malaysia: Bank Islam, Bank Muamalat Malaysia and MBSB Bank.[1] Similarly, among the investment banks, only KAF, Kenanga and MIDF Amanah are non-bank backed.[2] Thus, whilst in Malaysia 'universal bank' is not what Azman *et al.* (2019) refer to as a 'recognised legal term', the domestic banking system consists predominantly of large banking groups that offer both commercial and investment banking services.

In 2001, on the heels of the post-crisis bank restructurings, Bank Negara released its first *Financial Sector Masterplan*, serving as a ten-year 'change programme' (Bank Negara Malaysia 2001, 35). More specifically, the *Masterplan* spelled out phased recommendations for Malaysia's development and liberalisation of the banking sector, consisting of three phases. In phase 1, the capability and capacity of domestic institutions were to be strengthened, including through the encouragement of the ownership of banks by institutional investors (Bank Negara Malaysia 2001, 43). In phase 2, domestic competition was to be increased by levelling the playing field with incumbent foreign players. In phase 3, new foreign competition was to be introduced. Along these lines, and with some delay, in 2009 Bank Negara announced a series of financial liberalisation measures. This included the issuance of a limited number of new licences for commercial and Islamic banks, an increase in foreign equity limits up to 70 per cent for Islamic banks and investment banks as well as greater operational flexibility, for example with regard to the opening of new branches (Bank Negara Malaysia 2009).

The impact of bank consolidation on the financial system was significant. There was a sharp spike in bank concentration in the first decade

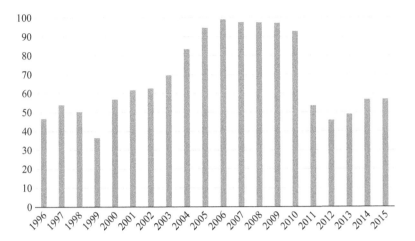

Figure 4.1 Bank concentration, 1996–2015 (percentage of total commercial banking assets)

Note: Assets of the three largest commercial banks as a share of total commercial banking assets.

Source: World Bank, *Global Financial Development Database* (Series GFDD. OI.01)

following the bank consolidation as Figure 4.1 illustrates. Liberalising measures introduced in 2009 contributed to more competition and an associated relative decline in concentration. Nevertheless, the market share held by Malaysia's three biggest banks – Maybank, CIMB and Public Bank – puts them in the category of what has become known, in post-global financial crisis terminology, as domestic systemically important banks (D-SIBs).[3] This has significant implications, including with regard to the scope for product innovation as I will discuss below with a focus on value-based intermediation.

Indeed, in the period under observation, Malaysia has been somewhat reluctant to liberalise the conventional banking sector and instead been significantly more pro-active in pursuing the liberalisation of the Islamic banking sector. Malaysia's first Islamic bank, Bank Islam Malaysia Berhad (BIMB) was established in 1983, shortly after Prime Minister Mahathir Mohamad had come into office. Malaysia's Pilgrimage Fund, Tabung Haji, contributed 12.5 per cent of its initial capital (Ariff 1988, 200).[4] For the first decade of its existence, Bank Islam was granted a quasi-monopoly. In 1993, Bank Negara introduced an 'interest-free banking scheme' and thus allowed other banks to open

Islamic 'windows' and to offer Islamic products and services. At the eve of the Asian financial crisis, the share of Islamic finance in the overall financial system was still relatively small (Warde 2000, 127). This should change dramatically in its aftermath, with Islamic finance coming to play an increasingly significant role in the Malaysian financial system.

Islamic finance featured prominently in the *Financial Sector Masterplan* (Bank Negara Malaysia 2001, ch. 5). In the *Masterplan*, Bank Negara set a target for Islamic finance to reach a share of 20 per cent of the banking sector by 2010. It also outlined a range of activities to promote Malaysia as an Islamic financial centre. In 2002, Bank Negara asked conventional banks to transform their Islamic windows into subsidiaries (Ariff 2017).[5] In so doing, Islamic banking was put onto a more solid footing, also in anticipation of the further opening up of the sector. In 2004, Bank Negara issued three new licences for Islamic banks to foreign Islamic financial institutions. The Financial Sector Blueprint adopted an even more ambitious Islamic finance agenda of 40 per cent in line with the target of the Economic Transformation Programme (Bank Negara Malaysia 2011, 47). Maybank's decision to adopt an 'Islamic first' strategy in 2010, offering its customers Islamic financial products and services per default, has to be understood in this context; Malaysia's second biggest bank, CIMB, followed suit. However, in so doing, Islamic finance became increasingly entangled with rising levels of household debt. Indeed, as I will discuss in more detail in the next section, the distinctive corporate ownership structure of Malaysian banks has played a significant role in the coalescing of state-permeated capitalism and socially suboptimal financialisation.

Financialisation dynamics in the Malaysian banking sector

In the two decades since the Asian financial crisis, the share of the financial system in the economy has expanded significantly, both as a percentage of GDP and in terms of employment. Thus, during the period of the Financial Sector Masterplan (2001–2010), the financial sector increased its role in the economy from 9.7 per cent of GDP in 2001 to 11.7 per cent of GDP in 2010 (Bank Negara Malaysia 2011, 26). Despite or perhaps rather because of the bank consolidations discussed in the previous sub-section, the level of state-permeation of the banking system remains high. Table 4.2 presents data on the largest shareholders of selected Malaysian banks. GLICs remain the single most important category of investors in the Malaysian domestic banking sector. Indeed, if we compare the data presented here, with the ownership structure of

Table 4.2 GLIC shareholdings in selected Malaysian banking groups (in per cent)

	EPF	KWAP	LTAT	PNB/ Schemes	Khazanah	Tabung Haji
Affin Bank	6.8		47.8*	1.1		
Alliance Bank Malaysia	9.9	1				
AmBank	6.9	2.5		7.6		
CIMB Bank	14.3	6.7		12.2	24.6	
Hong Leong Bank	2.3	1.4				
Maybank	12.5	4.7		48.7		
Public Bank	14.6	4.1		3.2		
RHB Bank	41.7	3.5		5.9		
Bank Islam	12	2.7		16.2		53
Bank Muamalat Malaysia	6.6+			1	30	1.8+
MBSB Bank	64.5				0.6	

Source: see Appendix A; figures calculated from top 15 shareholders, rounded to 1 decimal
Notes: *Directly and indirectly through Boustead Holdings Berhad
+ Indirectly through DRB-HICOM

key commercial banks in 2013 as compiled by Gomez *et al.* 2015 (cited in Gomez 2017, 110), then it is remarkable how little has changed, notwithstanding the 2018 regime change. Nevertheless, the ascendance of big banks in Malaysian capitalism is also clearly visible if we look, for example, at their increased weight in the economy. Indeed, as of June 2020, 7 out of 30 companies in the FTSE Bursa Malaysia KLCI, an index of the top 30 publicly listed companies, were banks, with a net market capitalisation of RM142 billion and a weight of 30.84 per cent (FTSE Russell 2020; see also Lau and Nur Zulaikha 2020, 6).

Malaysia's distinctive configuration of state-permeated capitalism, in particular government-linked shareholdings in the banking sector, intersect with – and at times exacerbate – financialisation dynamics in several ways. Whilst there exists a significant *potential* pool of domestic patient capital in Malaysia, in terms of performance expectations much of it is actually rather short-term. This has to be understood in the context of the importance of the announcement of annual GLIC dividends as a device that legitimises Malaysia's ethnically stratified, state-capitalist developmental model. Examples abound of where the politics of dividends have held primacy over other considerations. For example, Tabung Haji, with 9.3 million depositors, in 2019 in the midst of a government bailout and significant restructuring, nevertheless declared a 1.25 per cent dividend, albeit the lowest in its history.[6] Similarly, in May 2020, Affin Group, majority-owned by LTAT, the armed forces pension fund, was considering a reduction of its dividend payments from the seven sen per share it had announced in December of the previous year down to five sen in a bid to preserve cash because of the coronavirus crisis.[7] The move was rejected by Bursa Malaysia, citing listing requirements.[8]

The need to provide dividend payments to institutional shareholders is widely acknowledged among Malaysian banks as the framework within which they operate. This has an impact on their time horizons and discourages long-term investment in productive capacity. Once more, financialisation in Malaysia thrives on a combination of state intervention and ostensibly market-liberal practices. The result is a configuration of state-permeated capitalism, where the GLICs hold large, in a number of instances even controlling stakes in the domestic banks, but where at the same time the short-termism of a shareholder-value orientation prevails. This only underscores the country's complex politics of dividends. Nevertheless, this short-termism then exacerbates the mismatch that exists between short-term investor expectations, and the long-term maturity transformation that lending for the purpose of productive capacity-building necessitates. Figure 4.2 provides an overview of GLIC dividends since the Asian crisis. It furthermore illustrates that these have been higher, at times quite substantially so, than current deposit rates. Indeed, deposit rates have been hovering slightly above the 3 per cent mark in the period since the Asian crisis, apart from a short dip down to 2 per cent during the global financial crisis. Malaysia's distinctive politics of dividends thus feed into financialisation dynamics and vice versa.

Lending patterns have also shifted, away from corporate loans and towards the household sector. In fact, the last two decades have witnessed an unprecedented boom in household lending in Malaysia. In the aftermath of the Asian crisis, banks were encouraged to grow their loan books. For 1998 and 1999, Bank Negara set an annual target of 8 per cent loan growth. According to Chin (2005, 135), 'these measures not only failed to ensure increased productive sector bank borrowing, but instead encouraged the recurrence of a build-up of loans for unproductive activities'. He further points out that historically, there had been little government emphasis on encouraging investment in productive capacity such as manufacturing (Chin and Jomo 2000, 314; Chin 2005, 134).

Literature on universal banking tends to focus on the shift from industrial lending to investment banking, without doubt influenced

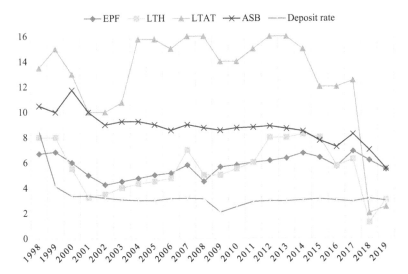

Figure 4.2 GLIC historical dividend rates over deposit rates (in per cent)

Note: Includes bonus and special dividends as applicable.

Sources: for GLIC dividends: EPF; MyPF (ASB); LTH & newspaper clippings; LTAT & newspaper clippings; for deposit rate: World Bank (Series FR.INR.DPST)

by a focus on analyses of the banking systems in the US and Europe. However, widening the empirical perspective demonstrates the importance of taking changes in household finances into account – and what they mean in terms of banks' business models (Ertürk and Solari 2007). The shift towards consumer finance and household lending, already observable prior to the Asian crisis, became significantly more pronounced in its aftermath as Figure 4.3a/b illustrates.

A large proportion of the growing volume of household loans has been due to the purchase of residential property, but loans are also being taken out to invest in the capital market, including to purchase unit trust certificates, a point to which I will return in Chapter 5. Indeed, the ability to borrow has become an increasingly important factor in explaining wealth inequalities in Malaysia, although the impact of the COVID-19 pandemic on property prices is yet uncertain. Capturing some of these effects, Bank Negara has begun to draw a distinction between 'loans for wealth accumulation' (residential and non-residential property and securities) and 'loans for consumption purposes' (motor vehicles, personal financing and credit cards), with the former increasing

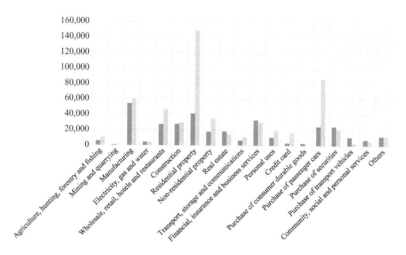

Figure 4.3a Bank lending by sector, December 1996 and 2005 (RM million)

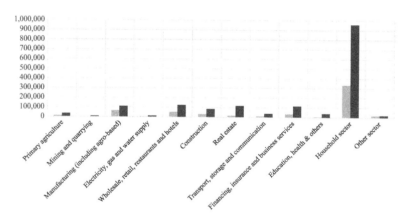

Figure 4.3b Bank lending by sector, December 2006 and 2018 (RM million)

Note: The comparability of the two figures is limited, given changes in loan classification categories.

Source: Bank Negara Malaysia, *Monthly Highlights and Statistics* (Series II.7 and 1.20)

at a much higher rate than the latter – 6.9 per cent versus 0.6 per cent in 2018 (Bank Negara Malaysia 2020b, 13).

At the same time, the Malaysian market for consumer lending has been very competitive, putting pressure on banks' earnings and acting as a significant driver of the international ambitions of Malaysian banks. Along these lines, the interest rate spread – that is the lending rate minus the deposit rate, or the difference between what the bank charges for a loan and what it pays for deposits – has steadily declined from a relative peak of 4.4 per cent in 1999 until bottoming out at 1.4 per cent in 2015.[9] By comparison, in 2019, in Indonesia it still stood at 3.7 per cent, as compared to 1.9 per cent in Malaysia. In the two decades since the Asian crisis, Malaysian domestic banking groups have developed a strong regional and, indeed, increasingly global presence. If, in 2002, total overseas assets stood at RM3.3 billion, by 2010, this had increased to RM240.2 billion. Similarly, the overseas contribution to pre-tax profit rose from RM108.9 million in 2002 to RM2.3 billion in 2010 during the period of the Financial Sector Masterplan (Bank Negara Malaysia 2011, 32). The international expansion of Malaysian banks thus has to be understood in the context of the pressure on profits exerted by an increasingly competitive home market, in combination with high dividend expectations as discussed above. In their expansion, Malaysian banks have focused on regional markets – Southeast Asia and greater China, also to follow their clients and support the expansion plans of non-financial companies. More recently, the GCC has also come increasingly in their purview; for example, Maybank Islamic launched its first branch in Dubai in 2019.

Nevertheless, it is important to note that this holds true for only a small number of Malaysian banks that have sought to adapt their business models to the increasingly competitive environment in this way. Some banks have also explored merger options. Perhaps among the most noteworthy of these were plans in 2015 for the creation of a mega-bank through the merger of CIMB, Malaysian Building Society and RHB that ultimately were not pursued. Likewise, there was discussion of a merger between AmBank and RHB in 2017 that also was abandoned, with sources citing AmBank's lingering exposure to the 1MDB scandal as a factor.[10]

Thus, among the Malaysian banks, Maybank and CIMB have been most proactive in expanding their regional footprint, facilitated by an increasingly outward looking regulatory approach, including with regard to participation in international regulatory networks and initiatives. The result is an increasingly stratified banking system with a small number of regional players, who have begun to actually export financialisation dynamics to new markets in terms of their operations and management, and domestic banks that face growing headwinds from competition.

Creating purpose? The challenges of value-based intermediation

Despite the very real financialisation dynamics in the Malaysian banking sector, Bank Negara governors have consistently emphasised the importance of situating finance in relation to the real economy. Thus, for the current planning period, Bank Negara (2011, 7) suggests that '[i]n this Blueprint, the growth of the financial sector will be firmly anchored to the growth of the real economy'. In this regard, there is widespread agreement that Islamic finance, with its principled approach to finance and asset-orientation, plays an important part in connecting finance with the real economy. For example, according to Zeti (2012a, 1), 'Islamic finance draws its strength from serving the real economy', in particular as financial transactions 'must be accompanied by an underlying economic transaction'. In the period since the Asian financial crisis, the share of Islamic finance in the banking system has increased steadily, both in absolute and relative terms (see Figure 4.4). Has the growth of Islamic finance therefore left an imprint on credit patterns? And how can it be reconciled with the financialisation dynamics highlighted in the previous section?

If we compare the lending patterns of Islamic and conventional banks, using data from Bank Negara's *Monthly Highlights and Statistics* (series 1.20), then there clearly are some differences, but these are perhaps not as pronounced as one would expect. Importantly, the shift towards lending to the household sector has been significant for both types of banks. Accordingly, rather than developing new types of risk-sharing, like their conventional counterparts, the Islamic banks have actually been focusing on what Ariff (2017, 9) calls 'to minimise risk'. Currently, the level of household debt as a percentage of GDP in Malaysia is among the highest in emerging market economies, albeit somewhat reduced from its 2015 peak of 89.1 per cent of GDP (Bank Negara Malaysia 2016, 14). This is in spite of Islamic injunctions against using debt as a source of profit. Moreover, with regard to the purpose of financing, in both absolute and relative terms, Islamic banks lend less to the manufacturing sector than conventional commercial banks. And whilst in absolute figures they are far behind conventional banks when it comes to lending to the household sector (RM319 billion versus RM637 billion as of December 2018), as a share of total loans, they are actually more exposed to it (60 per cent versus 56 per cent in December 2018).

In assessing levels of household debt, for Bank Negara the purpose of debt is an important criterion. This is underpinned by the

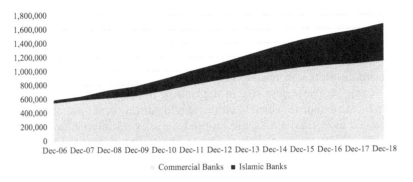

Figure 4.4 Total loans by type of bank (RM million)
Source: Bank Negara Malaysia, *Monthly Highlights and Statistics* (Series 1.20)

assumption, at least implicitly so, that the value of an asset will match or exceed the debt incurred in its purchase. Along these lines, housing is the largest single item that has driven household debt; and house prices in Malaysia have indeed been going up, at least prior to the COVID-19 pandemic. Nevertheless, there are larger moral questions that could be asked. For instance, given that speculation is prohibited in Islamic finance, is it then permissible to buy a house in an overheating and increasingly speculative property market? And what about socio-economic justice in a system where property has become seriously unaffordable in the major conurbations as highlighted in Bank Negara's own 2016 *Annual Report* (Bank Negara Malaysia 2017, 90–98; see also Rethel *et al.* (2019) for a critical discussion)? Likewise, Lee and Muhammed (2020, 29) identify increases in the value of higher-end property as an important indicator of the widening of wealth inequality in Malaysia.

As this example demonstrates, financialisation dynamics can contribute to a socially suboptimal allocation of credit, not just *across* sectors, as discussed with regard to trade-offs between investment in productive capacity versus financing of consumption, but also *within* sectors. Thus, not only does the Malaysian housing sector suffer from asset price inflation, but private developers have also tended to focus on more upscale developments in the RM500,000 and above category.[11] The result has been an oversupply of houses in the non-affordable price category and an undersupply of affordable housing. Moreover, in the context of Malaysia, most new properties sold by developers are bought off-plan, which creates its own problems.[12] For example, the question of how to deal with failure of delivery (on time) has been a major headache for Islamic banks, including their Shariah advisors.

According to Bank Negara's *Monthly Highlights and Statistics*, more specifically its data on 'classification of loans by sector' (series 1.20), the one sector where Islamic banks outperform conventional banks in both absolute and relative terms is loans to 'health care, education and other'. Nevertheless, like in the case of housing, bigger questions, such as the extent to which health care and education should be public goods or monetised assets, are ignored. In a recent intervention, Paul Langley (2020) argues that in the wake of the global financial crisis of 2008 political economy analysis has been overly focused on speculative logics and credit-debt relations. This, according to Langley, ignores another important dynamic crucial to the making of contemporary financialised capitalism, namely assetisation which he defines as 'the contingent processes which turn all manner of things into assets'.

In this regard, Chan (2013, 162–167) carefully details how health care in Malaysia has increasingly been turned into an investible asset, at both the federal and state level. Table 4.3 lists the largest shareholders in Malaysia's two main private healthcare groups. Chan (2013, 165–166) points to conflicts of interest the Malaysian state may face in its dual role of major healthcare provider (via Ministry of Health facilities) and as a major shareholder in the healthcare sector. This also has to be seen in the context of medical claims inflation, with price rises in Malaysia being above the global average, and also higher than in other Southeast Asian countries – including Indonesia, Singapore and Thailand (Bank Negara Malaysia 2020a, 41).[13] In other words, when it comes to realising the ethical potential of Islamic banking, or indeed, any type of financing, purpose cannot be understood in isolation from context. In contemporary global financial markets, this includes dynamics of assetisation and asset-price inflation and their role in financialised capitalism.

Table 4.3 Substantial shareholders in major healthcare providers (in per cent)

KPJ Holdings	*IHH Healthcare*
Johor Corporation – 38.7	MBK Healthcare Management/ Mitsui & Co. – 32.9
EPF – 12.2	Pulau Memutik Ventures/ Khazanah – 26
Waqaf An-Nur Corporation – 7.1	EPF – 8.2
KWAP – 5.4	Mehmet Ali Aydinlar – 5.9
PNB/ASB – 5	–

Sources: KPJ website; IHH *Annual Report 2019*

Ariff (2017, 8) suggests that the leading role of Islamic subsidiaries, as opposed to what he terms 'wholesome Islamic banks', in growing the market 'means that Islamic banks may stay focused on or remain preoccupied with producing "Shariah-compliant" products instead of venturing into the world of "Shariah-based" products'. In this regard, the state developmentalist agenda for Islamic finance, in combination with the 'Islamic first' strategies adopted by the country's major banks, may be something of a double-edged sword. On the one hand, it has played a significant role in the successful embedding of Islamic finance throughout the banking system. For example, industry observers point to the importance of the introduction of Islamic windows in the 1990s in giving Islamic finance customers access to much larger networks of bank branches and ATM facilities (Ariff 2017, 7). Regulatory Islamic finance targets and corporate Islamic-first strategies generated further momentum, but resulted in the taking to market of Islamic financial products that effectively replicate the product range of conventional banks.

Therefore, on the other hand, concerns have been raised that a focus on product replication, albeit in a Shariah-compliant manner, limits opportunities for Islamic finance to realise its potential as true alternative (Ariff 2017, 8). One often cited example is the lack of risk-sharing products in the Malaysian market. In this regard, the size of the major players in the Malaysian Islamic banking market can work as a constraint on the innovation of socially purposeful products given that they are systemically important – that is, their activities can impact the stability of the financial system. These constraints are amplified by an international regulatory context that favours debt over equity as enshrined in the risk-weighted approach to capital adequacy endorsed under the Basel regime.[14] In this regard, the impact of the new D-SIB framework remains to be seen. In other words, bank consolidation and Islamic bank subsidiarisation have had unintended, mutually reinforcing consequences in terms of narrowly demarcating the scope for socially purposeful finance. This is on top of the structural constraints posed by Malaysia's distinctive configuration of state shareholdership of banks and related profit expectations discussed in the previous section.

In fact, there have been some efforts to push Islamic banks in a more purposeful direction. In 2017, Bank Negara released for consultation a strategy paper on value-based intermediation (VBI). It built on months-long meetings with a group of Islamic banks depicted as a 'community of practitioners' in the paper. The aims of VBI include to chart the way towards a future financial landscape where innovation creates 'values for all' rather than mainly 'competitive advantage for shareholders and players' (Bank Negara Malaysia 2018, 10). Whilst the VBI framework was initially targeted at Islamic banks, throughout the process Bank Negara has emphasised its implications for the wider financial sector. In 2018, Bank Negara published the VBI Impact Assessment Framework and the VBI Scorecard. The former allows banks to assess the economic, social and environmental impacts of loan applications, whereas the latter is a management tool that allows Islamic banks to score their progress with regard to implementing VBI (Nor Shamsiah 2018).

In working with the Global Alliance for Banking on Values, Bank Negara could claim credibility at a time when the fallout from the 1MDB scandal was still fresh on everyone's mind. Nevertheless, to date, the impact of VBI has been somewhat mixed. The VBI initiative has been very successful as an awareness-raising measure. Moreover, in its wake, Islamic banks have made their social impact much more integral to their operations. At the same time, the VBI initiative has had little bearing on the context within which Malaysia's Islamic banks operate and that so significantly impacts the time horizon of their business operations. Along these lines, whilst VBI has contributed to product innovation, this has largely been within the existing focus on consumer finance, note for example the proliferation of 'rent-to-own' housing finance products.

Building on the value-based intermediation initiative, there has also been a growing focus on what policymakers refer to as 'social finance'. In the context of Malaysia, this term primarily refers to the charitable dimension of Islamic finance, including *zakat* (obligatory alms), *sadaqah* (charitable donations) and *waqf* (endowment). Along these lines, the central bank has announced that social finance will feature prominently in its next *Blueprint* to be released in 2021 (Bank Negara 2020a, 2, 34). The extent to which a focus on social finance will act on the recognition that the benefits from financial development initiatives have been spread very unevenly, an issue that a focus on 'access' as discussed in Chapter 2 fails to meaningfully address, is to be seen. This is so especially in the context of rising wealth inequality within ethnic groups in Malaysia, which remains a politically sensitive topic (Muhammed 2014; Lee and Muhammed 2020). Indeed, whilst for five decades the NEP has served as an important legitimation device of redistribution across ethnic lines, redistribution within ethnic groups has largely been a political taboo.[15] In this sense, a focus on social finance might have the potential to move the debate onto new terrain.

Conclusion

The period in the wake of the Asian financial crisis saw significant changes in the Malaysian financial system. The financial authorities, most importantly the central bank – Bank Negara Malaysia – spearheaded a number of reforms aimed at the consolidation of the banking system. As a result, the number of financial institutions in Malaysia declined. Nevertheless, with a reduction in the number of banks came an increase not only in the market share of the remaining institutions, but also in the reach of their range of activities with a much greater emphasis on consumer finance. This has been the case for both commercial banks and Islamic banks, and indeed many of the latter started out as windows of the former.

In Malaysia, changes in the banking sector have accentuated financialisation dynamics. Domestic institutional investors, more specifically government-linked investment companies, are the single largest group of investors in the banks. Given the politically sensitive nature of the dividends that these institutions declare, they expect market returns on their equity positions. In so doing, they do not act as providers of patient capital, but rather embed a synchronic investment logic in the Malaysian financial system. Overall, financialisation has thrived on a combination of state intervention and market-liberal reforms. The transformation of the banking system also had significant implications for capital markets with changes in the two sectors mutually reinforcing each other.

Notes

1 *The Edge Weekly* (17 April 2018).
2 *The Edge* (30 June 2015); see also Appendix A for more information on GLIC shareholdings in Malaysian banks.
3 In February 2020, Bank Negara Malaysia released its D-SIB framework (Bank Negara Malaysia Press Release, 5 February 2020). Effective as of 31 January 2021, it stipulates a higher loss absorbency requirement ranging from 0.5 per cent to 1 per cent.
4 Since then, it has replaced the Malaysian government as Bank Islam's largest shareholder, holding a share of over 50 per cent as of May 2020 (see also the information on bank shareholders provided in Appendix A).
5 *The Star* (31 October 2005).
6 *The Malaysian Reserve* (28 January 2020).
7 LTAT is both directly invested in Affin Bank and also majority shareholder of Boustead Holdings Berhad, which in turn is the third largest shareholder in Affin Bank (see also the information about bank shareholders in Appendix A).
8 *The Star* (9 May 2020).
9 World Bank (Series FR.INR.LNDP).
10 *The Star* (26 August 2017). The article also suggested that Bank Negara was a driving force behind the merger plans. Bank Negara (27 August 2017) reacted with a press release, claiming the article was 'inaccurate and

could cause confusion'. It further stated that 'mergers in the banking sector are mainly driven by the business considerations of banking institutions themselves', a claim that contrasts with the post-Asian crisis bank consolidations discussed earlier in this chapter.

11 *Malay Mail* (18 October 2016).

12 *The Edge* (9 July 2018).

13 Similarly, a growing offering range of education-related products and advice are clearly targeted at better-off customers, in particular those interested in sending their children to private and overseas universities. In addition to significant inflationary pressures in particular with regard to overseas university education, this further entrenches disparities of opportunity and wealth. Nevertheless, the case of education finance is especially intriguing, given the role of ethnic quotas in university admissions and scholarships. It points to differences in how processes of financialisation are unfolding among elites both within and outside Malaysia's ethnically stratified state.

14 See also Bortz and Kaltenbrunner (2018, 388) for a discussion of Basel III in the context of the financialisation of emerging economies.

15 Even calls to shift towards a system of 'needs-based' rather than 'race-based' affirmative action, as most prominently voiced by Anwar Ibrahim, have only made limited headway (see e.g. *New Straits Times*, 26 July 2019).

5 Financial deepening and the development of the capital market

The Asian crisis gave new momentum to capital market reforms, resulting in efforts to both deepen and widen the market. Since the early days of the implementation of the NEP, the capital market had played a strategic role in the restructuring of the economy. In the aftermath of the late 1990s crisis, its growth orientation became more pronounced. The previous chapter discussed reforms in the banking sector. In the wake of the Asian crisis, there was renewed recognition of the dangers of over-reliance on the banking sector, particularly in light of a spike in non-performing loans. As a consequence, financial risk and its diversification increasingly became a concern for financial elites. In this regard, capital market development, more specifically the development of bond and *sukuk* markets, was rendered as a market-friendly, unambiguous solution to volatile international capital flows.

Islamic finance has played a key role in both the deepening and widening of the capital market. On the one hand, Islamic finance enhances the range of financial instruments. On the other hand, it also increases the range of borrowers and investors. In fact, the expansion of Islamic finance was also seen as a way of tapping into new pools of liquidity – Malaysia was the first country to issue a global sovereign sukuk in 2002. The government has played a key role in developing the market. This has been not just through regulatory support, but also in its capacity as a market actor, providing the emerging sukuk market with benchmarks and liquid assets through the issuance of government, corporate and even multilateral Islamic debt securities. This includes Islamic debt issued by the government itself (Government Investment Issues), by government-linked companies (Khazanah) and by an international organisation in whose establishment it has played a crucial role (International Islamic Liquidity Management Corporation).[1] Further efforts to widen the capital market have also seen increased support for the development of the investment management industry. Nevertheless, throughout this period, financialisation dynamics also intensified and accentuated inequalities of wealth.

This chapter is divided into three parts. The next section looks in more detail at efforts to develop domestic capital markets in the wake of the Asian crisis. The section thereafter will examine financialisation dynamics in the capital market. The third section will then focus specifically on attempts to develop frameworks for sustainable and responsible investment, which gained greater momentum in the wake of the Paris Agreement and UN Sustainable Development Goals. In Malaysia, these frameworks have received high-level attention as they are seen as complementary to the country's Islamic finance ambitions, although take-up on the ground has been somewhat muted.

Widening and deepening the capital market

At the time of the outbreak of the Asian crisis, the size of the Malaysian stock market, measured in terms of market capitalisation as a percentage of GDP, was among the deepest in the world.[2] By comparison, the bond market, albeit one of the bigger ones in Asia, was still small. In 1997, the nominal value of bonds outstanding was less than RM120 billion, whereas the market capitalisation of the Kuala Lumpur Stock Exchange had reached more than RM800 billion (Bank Negara Malaysia 1999, 634–635). One of the reasons for this divergence had been that much of the credit growth associated with the privatisation drive of the late 1980s and early 1990s had been channelled through the banking system (Bank Negara Malaysia 2001, 103). In the wake of the Asian crisis, the development of the bond market became a key priority for financial policymakers. The spike in non-performing loans at the height of the crisis had illustrated to policymakers the dangers of over-reliance on the banking sector and the need to diversify financing (Government of Malaysia 1999, 20). Moreover, the specific way in which financial restructurings took place – the acquisition of NPLs and bank recapitalisations were financed through the issuance of bonds – highlighted the importance of a well-functioning bond market.

In June 1999, the National Bond Market Committee (NBMC) was established to 'provide the overall policy direction' for bond market development and 'rationalise the regulatory framework' (Salleh 2002, 149). Its membership comprised representatives from Bank Negara, the Securities Commission, EPU, the Registrar of Companies and the Kuala Lumpur Stock Exchange. It was chaired by the Secretary-General of the Treasury. Its various subcommittees were tasked with looking into regulatory reform, product innovation and infrastructure development.

On the recommendation of the NBMC, the Securities Commission was declared the sole regulator of the corporate bond market with effect from July 2000. In 2001, after extensive consultations with market practitioners, the Securities Commission released its first *Capital Market Masterplan*. In the Plan, it set itself targets with regard to the liberalisation, development and internationalisation of the Malaysian capital market (Securities Commission 2001). This included opening up the market to foreign borrowers, including multilateral institutions and multinational corporations (Zeti 2012b).

The financial crisis of 1997–1998 presented a turning point in that it gave rise to a greater emphasis on (capital market) institution building within Malaysia's market paradigm. In particular, the crisis highlighted the need for corporate governance reform. Since 1999, Malaysia has formulated a substantial range of initiatives in this regard. This includes various initiatives to strengthen the institutional framework, such as the introduction of the Malaysian Code of Corporate Governance (MCCG) and the establishment of the Minority Shareholder Watchdog Group in 2000. The MCCG has been reviewed several times, 2007, 2012 and most recently in 2017. In 2011, the Securities Commission published its *Corporate Governance Blueprint*, in line with the governance focus of its second *Capital Market Masterplan* (Securities Commission 2011). Nevertheless, as it is succinctly stated in CMP2, '[c]orporate governance remains very much work-in-progress in Malaysia' (Securities Commission 2011, 78). This included, according to the Securities Commission (2011, 79) a tendency among publicly listed companies 'to comply with the form, rather than substance of corporate governance codes'. Overall Malaysia's corporate governance landscape remains characterised by close ties between politics and business, exacerbated by the prominence of GLCs among the publicly listed companies and their government-linked investors.

In addition to deepening the market, there have also been significant efforts to widen it, foremost focused on the development of Islamic capital markets. By now, Islamic finance is widely recognised as an asset class, but that was by no means the case at the time of the Asian crisis. In its wake, the promotion of Islamic finance was a means to legitimise Malaysia's developmental project, in particular among the Malay community, in the face of the fallout from the crisis. Moreover, it was seen as a way to tap new pools of liquidity at a time when international investors still considered the Malaysian market with caution, following the imposition of temporary capital controls in 1998 (Lai *et al.* 2017). In 2001, Kumpulan Guthrie issued the first ever global corporate sukuk.[3] In 2002, the Government of Malaysia followed suit, issuing the first global sovereign sukuk and paving the way for future sovereign and corporate issuances. To support the market, the regulatory framework for sukuk was strengthened further. In 2004, the Securities Commission issued its *Guidelines on the Offering of Islamic Securities* and in 2009 its *Registration of Shariah Advisers Guidelines*.

Likewise, in the aftermath of the Asian crisis, Malaysian financial policymakers put significant efforts into improving the country's standing in international regulatory networks, in order to 'maintain an *effective voice* in future international capital market development' (Securities Commission 2001, 18, my emphasis). Along these lines, the Securities Commission has very actively cultivated its external relationships and become an important node in the regional and international governance of capital markets. Over the years, the Securities Commission came to play a significant role in IOSCO, in particular – but not only – with regard to Islamic finance.[4] In 2016, IOSCO approved the establishment of its first ever regional office, the IOSCO Pacific Asia Hub in Kuala Lumpur, aimed at offering capacity building activities for Asian regulators. Similarly, the Securities Commission has also developed a significant presence in regional regulatory networks, in particular the ASEAN Capital Markets Forum, which I will discuss in more detail below in the context of the development of regional green bond standards. Moreover, the Securities Commission engages in various bilateral cooperation and knowledge exchange schemes, including with regulators in Asia and the Middle East. Once more, this illustrates the dense web of relationships that underpins the development of capital markets.

Financialisation dynamics in the Malaysian capital market

Since the Asian crisis, much of the growth in the capital market has been driven by bonds and increasingly sukuk, bond-like financial instruments that are structured in a way that makes them Shariah-compliant. Essentially, bonds are debt certificates specifying the relationship between creditor and debtor. What distinguishes bond debt from the other major form of debt provided by the formal financial system, bank loans, is that bonds are easily transferable. Through bonds, a loan is broken up into smaller denominations and usually claims are marketable, meaning that they can be sold and bought in a secondary market. As a consequence, an intrinsic feature of bonds is that they are more liquid than traditional bank loans. In so doing, theoretically, bonds are especially well-suited to financing projects with a long gestation, including infrastructure projects or business expansions – the

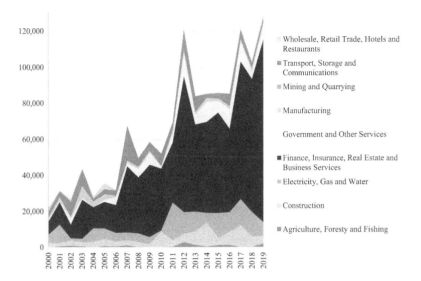

Figure 5.1 New issues of corporate bonds and *sukuk* by sector, 2000–2019 (RM million)

Source: Bank Negara Malaysia, *Monthly Highlights and Statistics* (Series 2.11)

so-called real economy. Nevertheless, Figure 5.1 shows new issues of corporate bonds and sukuk by sector of the issuer. By far the largest group of issuers of bonds are companies from the 'finance, insurance, real estate and business services' sector. Indeed, in the period from 2000 to 2019, the share of this sector in terms of volume of new issues rose from around one-third to over three-quarters.[5]

In fact, bond markets, in Asia and elsewhere, have historically been reliant on the state-led development of market infrastructures. Similarly, government-linked market actors and market-supporting institutions have played a crucial role in the construction of these markets, including with regard to the creation of demand and supply and the establishment of prices (Rethel and Sinclair 2014). Along these lines, the distinction between corporate and government bond markets is not as straightforward as it seems at first glance, and indeed, in Malaysia the corporate bond market exhibits a significant degree of state permeation. Among the bonds classified as corporate bonds in Malaysia, there are a sizeable number of government-guaranteed bonds, including bonds issued by infrastructure and public housing financiers (Danainfra, LPPSA) and the student loans company (PTPN). According to the Malaysian Bond and Sukuk Information Exchange database, government-guaranteed bonds constitute more than a quarter of corporate bonds outstanding.[6]

Similarly, GLICs have acted not only as investors, but also as corporate borrowers. This includes most prominently Khazanah (including via Danum Capital, Rantau Abang Capital, Danga Capital and Ihsan Sukuk), which has played a substantial role in market development by issuing benchmark-sized sukuk and pioneering new product structures, such as Malaysia's inaugural social impact sukuk. In so doing, Khazanah has been a reliable source of highly rated sukuk. At the same time, Khazanah's creditworthiness is 'premised on its critical link with the Government of Malaysia (GoM) and its fairly diversified investment portfolio that comprises strong credit profile investee companies and provide sustainable dividend earnings' as RAM Ratings (2018), one of Malaysia's two domestic rating agencies, succinctly puts it.[7] Likewise, some GLCs have a strong presence in the corporate bond market. This includes the domestic banks (and their SPVs), in particular CIMB and Maybank, which also tend to have higher debt-to-equity ratios than other Malaysian banks.[8]

The expansion of bond markets since the Asian crisis thus has to be viewed alongside the dynamics of ownership and control in the equity market and banking sector, which Gomez (2017) so forensically analysed. In this regard, bonds have the distinct advantage over equity that they do not dilute ownership. Hence, they serve as important conduits for attracting private portfolio capital, from both domestic and overseas investors. Indeed, in terms of raising new capital for the private sector, the bond market has outperformed the equity market in every year since the Asian crisis, with the exception of 2002 (Maxis IPO) and 2010 (a year of several 'blockbuster' IPOs, including Petronas Chemical Group).[9] Figure 5.2 shows net funds raised in the capital market since 1997, also reflecting redemptions of corporate bonds and sukuk. Likewise, in about a third of years, net funds raised by the private sector via bonds and sukuk exceeded funds raised by the public sector.[10]

On the investor side, once more, bond markets are far from atomistic, and lines between state and market, and public and private are blurred. Indeed, they espouse a similar logic of financialised state permeation. To a large extent, as previously discussed, institutional demand for securities is driven by the investment strategies and mandates of the GLICs, most importantly the EPF (Securities Commission 2011, 30–32).

In addition to mandatory pension savings, the cultivation of unit trust investment has a long tradition in Malaysia, going back to the early phase of the NEP, more specifically the incorporation of PNB in 1978

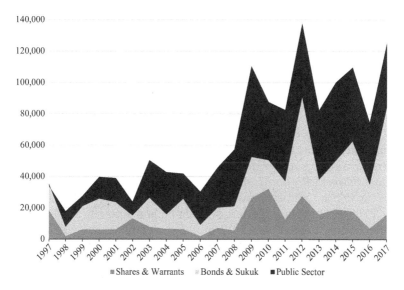

Figure 5.2 Net funds raised in the capital market, 1997–2017 (RM million)
Source: Bank Negara Malaysia, *Monthly Highlights and Statistics* (Series 2.10)

(Gomez and Jomo 1999, 35; Gomez 2017, 34–37). Following the introduction of the NEP, companies seeking to list on the stock exchange
had been mandated to make special share allocations to Bumiputera
investors (Gill 1985; Jesudason 1989; Gomez 2017, 34). However, it
soon emerged that the direct selling of shares to Bumiputeras did little
to affect corporate ownership patterns, given that these shares, bought
at a discount, were quickly sold on. Reacting to the failure of special
share allocations to individual Bumiputera investors, the government
created a network of organisations and trust agencies which directly
invested into companies and held shares on behalf of Bumiputeras
(Rethel 2010b, 501). PNB was created with the aim of acquiring shares
to be transferred to a trust in which individual Bumiputeras could
acquire units.

In 1981, PNB launched its first unit trust, Amanah Saham Nasional
(ASN). To encourage ASN take-up, a minimum return of 10 per cent
was guaranteed until 1990 (Rethel 2010b, 501). Following the success of
the scheme, another trust, Amanah Saham Berhad (ASB) was launched
in 1990. Since then, ASB has turned into the country's largest unit trust
(Lee and Muhammed 2020, 29). In 1996, PNB launched the first scheme
open to non-Malays. By 2019, PNB managed a total of 14 unit trusts

and one proprietary fund (PNB 2020, 43). The total number of PNB unit trust accounts had reached 14.3 million, with RM253 billion units in circulation (PNB 2020, 12–13). In so doing, PNB has played a significant role in the practice of unit trust investment becoming widely adopted in Malaysia.

Nevertheless, the rise of unit trust investment has also (literally) compounded inequalities of wealth (Muhammed 2014, 24–25; Lee and Muhammed 2020, 29–30).[11] We can see this for the case of PNB trusts, but even more so with regard to the growth of the unit trust industry more generally as I will show below. In line with its mandate to provide alternative savings vehicles for Bumiputera (and thus widen access to the capital market), PNB's flagship ASB fund has an individual subscription cap in place for new units being released, which currently stands at RM200,000. However, with just over ten million accounts and RM167 billion units in circulation in 2019, average holdings are less than a tenth of the maximum allocation (PNB 2020, 133). This means that ASB, and the dividends it declares, is of the greatest benefit to the small number of Bumiputera investors able to buy in at the right time and maximise their allocation. The ability of some households to borrow loans to purchase securities, primarily ASB units, further compounds this, as well as 'bolster[ing]' household debt (Bank Negara Malaysia 2020b, 11).

Another important step undertaken in order to promote unit trust investment was the liberalisation of EPF savings. In 1996, the Members Investment Scheme (MIS) was introduced, to address shortfalls in pension savings and enable greater diversification. It allows EPF account holders to invest a share of their pension savings in unit trusts approved under the scheme.[12] The start of the EPF MIS, just before Malaysia was to be hit by the Asian crisis, was not very auspicious. Nonetheless, the scheme gained in popularity in the early 2000s, with a jump in the number of participating members in the wake of the global financial crisis (the EPF dividend had dipped from 5.8 per cent in 2007 to 4.5 per cent in 2008) (Agnes *et al.* 2011, 54; EPF 2020). In 2016 and 2017, a number of liberalisation measures were introduced. This included removing a foreign exposure cap of 30 per cent for eligible funds and raising the eligible amount EPF members could invest via MIS to 30 per cent (once an age-related threshold of savings has been achieved).[13]

Table 5.1 provides an overview of the growth of the unit trust industry in Malaysia. Since 2008, the net asset value of these funds has more than tripled, with particularly the Shariah-compliant share growing more than six-fold. In 2011, the net asset value of unit trust funds stood at 19.42 per cent as a percentage of Bursa Malaysia market capitalisation.[14] By 2020, it had reached 29.52 per cent. Similarly, the number

Table 5.1 Unit trust investment – overview

Year	Net Asset Value (RM bn)			Units in Circulation (RM bn)			No. of Launched Funds		
	Conventional	Shariah	Total	Conventional	Shariah	Total	Conventional	Shariah	Total
2008	114.3	16.1	130.4	187.5	48.9	236.4	392	140	532
2009	169.6	22.1	191.7	216.7	56.8	273.5	397	144	541
2010	202.8	24.0	226.8	232.8	56.2	288.9	412	152	564
2011	221.6	27.9	249.5	255.2	61.2	316.4	423	164	587
2012	259.5	35.4	294.9	281.7	69.9	351.6	420	169	589
2013	292.7	42.8	335.5	308.2	80.3	388.5	417	178	595
2014	296.4	46.7	343.0	330.8	94.6	425.4	424	188	612
2015	294.5	52.1	346.6	350.5	107.5	458.0	419	193	612
2016	297.6	60.9	358.5	368.7	128.2	496.9	429	198	627
2017	349.2	77.8	427.0	414.7	147.7	562.4	431	213	644
2018	342.7	83.5	426.2	457.2	172.0	629.2	426	224	650
2019	374.8	107.3	482.1	494.3	202.1	696.4	449	236	685
2020*	360.5	104.4	464.9	503.9	194.7	698.6	457	238	695

Note: excluding wholesale funds effective January 2009

* as at 31 May 2020

Source: Securities Commission, Unit Trust Fund Summary of Statistics, as at 31 December

of accounts had grown from just below 15.5 million to over 20 million accounts. Moreover, we can see a clear increase in the number of units in circulation coinciding with the liberalisation of EPF MIS. However, other factors might have also been at play. Thus, Syahirah *et al.* (2020, 241) highlight that recent scandals gave a boost to EPF MIS take-up as citizen investors were keen to move funds away from the EPF, viewing it 'as part of the government'. Nonetheless, these trusts are very much embedded within Malaysia's existing system of ownership and control, with the majority of EPF MIS approved unit trusts once more being bank-backed (Federation of Investment Managers Malaysia 2020).

By contrast, to date the introduction of a Private Retirement Scheme (PRS) in 2012 as a third, private pillar in the Malaysian pension system to complement EPF savings has been less successful. With a total net asset value of RM3.6 billion as of May 2020, PRS have stayed far behind the RM30.9 that they were expected to reach according to CMP2 projections (Securities Commission 2011, 35; Securities Commission 2020). In 2015, the investment management industry was further liberalised by introducing licences for boutique fund management companies, catering to high net worth clients and financial institutions. In so doing, in Malaysia, financial development, more specifically the introduction of a wider range of investment options, has further accentuated inequalities of wealth. Similar patterns have emerged in relation to 401(k) pension plans in the US and Individual Savings Accounts in the UK.

Efforts to promote the unit trust industry, and portfolio investment managers more broadly, have also taken on a regional dimension. In 2014, the Securities Commission, together with the Monetary Authority of Singapore and the Securities and Exchange Commission of Thailand launched the ASEAN Collective Investment Scheme (CIS) Framework. Subject to regulatory approval in both home and host countries, it allows unit trusts authorised in one participating jurisdiction to offer units to subscribers in other participating jurisdictions. However, in its first five years the take-up had been very limited, with fund managers citing difficulties to get approval and lack of demand as main obstacles.[15]

As the fate of capital markets has become an increasingly important means of signalling economic competence, their growth and prosperity are core concerns of government policy. Market interventions by domestic institutional investors have to be understood in this context. The lines have become increasingly blurred between actions being taken to shore up government interests or to protect a middle-class public that has become more directly exposed to the capital market. Overall, capital markets and their governance remain closely tied to the need for performance legitimacy. However, this is also where new fault lines have emerged, given a decline of trust in Malaysia's ethnically stratified version of state capitalism (see also Syahirah *et al.* 2020, 240–241).

The lack of publicly available data on wealth, indebtedness and inequality, in particular their breakdown along communal lines, necessitates corroboration from other sources, such as either available statistics that can be used as proxies (Lee and Muhammed 2020) or interviews (e.g. Syahirah *et al.* 2020). Since the Asian crisis, housing has been deemed a comparatively safer investment than direct investing in the stock market, contributing to imbalances in the housing market. Moreover, there seems to have been an emerging trend of funds being moved from GLICs to other providers, in response to declining trust in government institutions. This includes Tabung Haji account closures in the wake of the 1MDB scandal.[16] Similarly, Syahirah *et al.* (2020, 241) suggest that the popularity of the EPF Members Investment Scheme has also been due to a lack of trust in EPF itself. A growing number of Malaysians are also looking into investing overseas, such as UK property, including student accommodation.[17] There is thus growing pressure on GLICs to improve their performance to pre-empt wider challenges to Malaysia's institutional set-up. Recent calls for a new GLC transformation programme, and the appointment of experienced turnaround managers to key corporate and government positions, have to be seen in this context.[18] Moreover, like in the banking industry, there has also been greater interest in the social purpose of investment.

Sustainable and responsible investment: paradigm shift or elusive goals?

Since the early 2000s, socially responsible investing has gained global traction, boosted by the advocacy of the United Nations for integrating economic, social and governance (ESG) considerations into investment decisions. It got further momentum from the Paris Agreement on Climate Change and the Sustainable Development Goals, both adopted in 2015. The Paris Agreement and SDGs enshrine the move towards more sustainable investment in two important ways. First, they put an onus on financial institutions to create mechanisms that allow them to screen the finance they provide to ensure it is aligned with global climate and developmental goals. Along these lines, various schemes have emerged that financial institutions can join to demonstrate their commitment to principled finance approaches, including the Principles for Responsible Investment, the UNEP Finance Initiative and the Equator Principles (UN Global Compact no date). Second, these frameworks actively seek to create new markets through which to engage private finance in addressing global environmental and developmental challenges. For example, the financing gap for realising the SDGs alone is estimated to be in the range of US$2.5–3 trillion per year (as quoted in UKIFC and ISRA 2020, 12). There is wide agreement in the Islamic finance industry on the significant overlap between Islamic finance and these global environmental and developmental goals (Securities Commission 2019, 13). In this sense, the SDGs are seen as an 'opportunity' for Islamic finance to realise its ethical potential (UKIFC and ISRA 2020, 13–14).

In Malaysia, the promotion of socially responsible finance and investment already had been highlighted in CMP2 (Securities Commission 2011, 29). Efforts were stepped up in 2014, when the SC introduced its Sustainable and Responsible Investment (SRI) Strategy and issued its SRI Sukuk Framework. Incidentally, this was the same year that Malaysia introduced the Malaysian Sustainable Palm Oil Standard (MSPO), as an alternative framework to Roundtable on Sustainable Palm Oil (RSPO) certification (Nesadurai 2018, 223). Once more, GLICs played an important role in developing the market. Thus, for example, the inaugural social impact sukuk under the SRI Sukuk Framework was issued by Khazanah in 2015. There was also an anticipated greater demand for SRI assets, with EPF introducing its Shariah option in 2016 and SC promotion of SRI funds.[19]

Malaysia has also sought to use its position in the ASEAN Capital Market Forum to further its SRI agenda. In 2017, ACMF released its ASEAN Green Bond Standards, the first such framework that specifically references sukuk (ACMF 2017, 5). In the same year, the first corporate green sukuk had been issued in Malaysia to finance a solar power plant in Sabah. It was followed by the region's first sovereign green sukuk issued by the Republic of Indonesia in early 2018. The ASEAN Green Bond Standards were developed by ACMF during the chairmanship of Malaysia, with significant input from the World Bank, more specifically its Kuala Lumpur-based regional knowledge hub. Unlike in the case of palm oil, where the Malaysian state sought to develop an alternative framework to existing certification schemes, here the Securities Commission builds on its position in regional (and global) regulatory networks to mainstream these standards at the regional level. In 2017, an RM6 million Green SRI Sukuk grant scheme was established to further support the development of the market. Through these initiatives, Malaysia also seeks to leverage overlaps between Islamic finance and responsible and sustainable finance to enhance its position as a regional SRI centre (Securities Commission 2019, 17).

The development of Islamic capital markets is truly remarkable and its significant achievements should not be downplayed. At a time when financial markets have run footloose, Islamic finance unambiguously embraces a principled approach to finance. Moreover, given its post-colonial and, predominantly, Global South context, Islamic finance, developed from a structurally subordinate position, has nevertheless made significant inroads in global financial markets (Lai *et al.* 2017). However, Islamic finance has also struggled to realise its ethical objectives, not so much because of a certain business pragmatism, but because the question of how it can maximise its social impact is far from straightforward. Along these lines, the relationship between ESG and Islamic finance is more conflictual than is typically acknowledged. Some of this is due to the nature of ESG investment itself, more specifically the ambition of pursuing market-based solutions to collective action problems. But some of these frictions are also due to the way Islamic finance has evolved and the attempts that have been made to mainstream it. The following discussion will bring some of these value-conflicts to the fore.

Since its inception, the development of modern Islamic finance has been closely intertwined with the oil economy (Maurer 2005; El Gamal and Jaffe 2012). The experience of Malaysia has been a case in point. Indeed, landmark Islamic finance transactions have been tied to the fossil fuel sector and, more recently, palm oil. Just take the first ever corporate sukuk, issued by Shell Malaysia in 1990 to finance a plant producing gas-to-liquid products; or the first ever global corporate sukuk, issued by Malaysian Kumpulan Guthrie in 2001 to refinance the acquisition of a palm oil plantation in Indonesia. In this regard, a greater awareness of environmental issues signifies an important development in the industry. It is to be hoped that this will also contribute to more research that disentangles the industry's somewhat chequered history when it comes to environmental concerns.

Similarly, by its very nature, Islamic finance is concerned with social considerations, but it tends to regard only a somewhat narrow range of issues as being within its remit. Thus, the financing of socially harmful products such as alcohol or weapons is clearly prohibited. But on other social issues there exist substantial differences of opinion, for example pertaining to questions about the enforcement of labour standards. Moreover, despite women having played an important role in the development of the Islamic finance industry in Malaysia – as regulators, market practitioners and Shariah advisors – there is still a tendency to marginalise their views (Elder 2017). It raises concerns about both the substance and the extent of the sector's commitment to equity and justice. The absence of women's voices is very visible, for example, with regard to the significant underrepresentation of women speakers at Islamic finance industry conferences, including events that focus on overlap with SDGs. The irony in this, of course, is that to 'achieve gender equality and empower all women and girls' is one of the Sustainable Development Goals.

In the remainder of this section, I want to concentrate on two of the governance aspects of ESG – tax and remuneration. Once again, I will focus not on the purpose, but on the context in which the shift to ESG is taking place, more specifically the nexus between financialisation and widening inequalities. Although it was not initially considered as ESG-relevant, there is a growing consensus among academics and practitioners that tax is a critical aspect of governance, if not even wider ESG frameworks (see e.g. KPMG 2019; Paul and Stange 2020). However, this sits at odds with the development framework for capital markets in Malaysia. Tax incentives have played a significant role in the promotion of the capital market, including its Islamic components. At the same time, tax regimes can amplify financialisation dynamics, for example by favouring financial speculation over productive investment (Tomaskovic-Devey *et al.* 2015, 542–543).

The Malaysian tax regime generally favours capital market investment. There is no withholding tax on dividends and capital gains from stocks are tax-exempt (Deloitte 2018, 9). Stamp duty, set at 0.1 per cent, is capped at RM200 and in 2018 a three-year tax waiver for small- and mid-cap stocks was introduced.[20] Whilst there have been debates about extending capital gains tax to stocks, these tend to be short-lived.[21] The use of tax incentives is justified as being necessary for promoting the development of the capital market, including the sukuk market and the investment management industry. Overall, the result of these sorts of promotional activities is to reinforce the favourable tax treatment of portfolio investment as opposed to waged employment (taxed at up to 28 per cent) or even consumption (sales tax is set at 10 per cent, with a 5 per cent reduced rate).

Along these lines, a wide range of special incentives have been introduced in the Islamic capital market, including tax exemptions and the tax deductibility of certain costs (see Securities Commission no date, for an overview). Similarly, fiscal incentives are an important policy instrument when it comes to supporting Malaysia's ambition to develop the green and social finance sectors. This includes tax incentives for issuers of SRI sukuk and SRI funds as well as the tax exemption of the Green SRI Sukuk Grant scheme (Securities Commission 2019, 16). From a governance perspective, the use of tax incentives in supporting the nascent green and social finance markets is not without its downsides. In this regard, weaning the capital market from its dependence on tax incentives would achieve a more equal treatment of capital and labour and contribute to the sustainability of the government budget. This would also more closely align with Islamic taxation principles, and their focus on wealth rather than income.

Another governance aspect that deserves further attention is the issue of remuneration. Both Bank Negara and the Securities Commission have subscribed to the view that retaining and attracting 'talent' is crucial to the development of the financial sector, and indeed necessitates capital market growth. The somewhat circular logic of this sentiment is succinctly expressed in CMP2:

> In recent years, global competition for talent has intensified and Malaysian talent is highly sought after in many countries. Malaysia's high income strategy is clearly inter-linked with a strategy to attract and retain talent which requires narrowing the remuneration differential with international financial centres. This underscores the urgent need for high growth strategies for the Malaysian capital market to generate revenue growth to increase the capability to offer higher salaries to compete for talent.
>
> (Securities Commission 2011, 50)

At the same time, however, excessive remuneration practices in international financial centres such as the UK and the US have come under significant criticism following the fallout from the global financial crisis of 2008. In the 1MDB scandal, bonus culture certainly seems to have played a role in encouraging criminal behaviour and ethical misconduct in the capital market. A case in point are 1MDB bond issuances taken to market by the Singapore office of US investment bank Goldman Sachs. In 2012 and 2013, Goldman arranged three bond issues for 1MDB with a total face value of US$6.5 billion, for which it received US$600 million in fees, a multiple of the typical industry rate.[22] Much of the funds raised were later unaccounted for.[23]

In the Malaysian context, it has to be noted that the compensation of GLC CEOs is generally lower than that of their (more) private sector counterparts. This also holds true for the financial sector. Thus, for example, in 2018, with total compensation of RM7.3 million and RM8.7 million, respectively, the pay packages of the Group CEOs of Maybank and CIMB were significantly lower than the RM42.4 million received by the CEO of Public Bank.[24] Nevertheless, there has been little engagement with alternative frameworks for compensation, including with views presented in Islamic economics. This is in spite of questions of compensation being considered in Islamic economic thought, albeit under radically different premises. For example, Sayyid Abul Ala Mawdudi, widely credited for setting out the principles of modern Islamic economics, explicitly addressed questions of remuneration in his work – with recommendations that are far removed from today's financialised reality. It is worthwhile quoting him at length:

> The existing gap of over one to 100 in the remuneration ratio should be reduced for the time being to one to 20, and then gradually brought down to a level of one to 10. It should also be decided once for all that no remuneration will be less than the minimum level of wages necessary to satisfy the basic needs of an average family, according to the inflationary trend of that period. Thus, a continuous process of review will have to be followed to maintain the desired level of wages and remunerations.
>
> (Mawdudi 2011, 250)

Conclusion

In the wake of the Asian crisis of the late 1990s, significant efforts were undertaken to widen and deepen the Malaysian capital market. This included the development of the bond market and the significant expansion of the investment management industry. At the same time, however, Malaysia's model of ethnically stratified capitalism, and related dynamics of ownership and control, have been surprisingly stable. Thus, GLICs and GLCs are prominent borrowers and investors in the corporate bond market. Similarly, the majority of unit trusts, especially those that are part of the EPF Members Investment Scheme, are backed by the banks. In so doing, a rather distinctive form of state-permeated financialisation has emerged. Likewise, the development of the capital market has accentuated inequalities of wealth.

Globally, for most of the past 20 years, Malaysia has had by far the most developed Islamic capital market, in terms of both size and product range. The rise of ESG investment is seen as an opportunity in this regard, as many of its goals overlap with the greater objectives of Islamic finance. It is also something the Malaysian regulators and financial institutions have actively pursued. However, in terms of how market development unfolds, rather than offering a radical alternative, Islamic finance tends to shore up the status quo.

Notes

1 Another noteworthy entity in this regard is Cagamas, Malaysia's national mortgage corporation. Although not classified as a GLIC, it is part-owned by Bank Negara with a 20 per cent stake. Cagamas raises bonds and sukuk in the debt market to finance the purchase of housing loans and other receivables, primarily from financial institutions.

2 The market capitalisation of domestic listed companies had hit an all-time high of just above 320 per cent of GDP in 1993 (World Bank, Series CM.MKT.LCAP.GD.ZS).

3 PNB was the largest single shareholder of Kumpulan Guthrie following the 1981 Guthrie 'Dawn Raid', an important moment in Malaysia's post-colonial history.

4 It had joined IOSCO, the International Organization of Securities Commissions, shortly after its establishment in 1993. For example, IOSCO's 2004 *Islamic Finance Fact-Finding Report* was drafted with significant input from the Securities Commission. Similarly, the SC took a leading role in the 2011 IOSCO report *Development of Corporate Bond Markets in the Emerging Markets* (SC 2014, 211). In 2013, then-SC chairman Ranjit A. Singh became the chair of IOSCO's influential Emerging Markets Committee, since then renamed as the Growth and Emerging Markets Committee. It represents three quarters of IOSCO's membership, amongst them ten G-20 members.

5 Note, however, that the data provided in Figure 5.2 refers to the sector of the issuer, rather than the purpose of the funds. Included among the issuers are entities such as Danainfra and LPPSA, whose sole purpose is to finance infrastructure and public housing, respectively. Examining their role in both financial development and as development financiers goes beyond the scope of this book.

6 Bond and Sukuk Information Exchange database, author's calculation.

7 RAM Press Release (28 November 2018). According to the Bond and Sukuk Information Exchange database, further GLIC(-linked) borrowers include *de facto* GLIC Urusharta Jamaah, established to deal with underperforming assets previously owned by Tabung Haji and whose purchase was financed via the issuance of sukuk (*The Edge Weekly*, 12 May 2020), PNB through its Merdeka Ventures and, indeed, 1MDB debt.

8 A detailed breakdown of issuers can be found, for example, in the Bond and Sukuk Information Exchange database.

9 *The Edge* (15 November 2009); *The Edge* (27 December 2010).

10 This includes as part of the public sector Khazanah bonds issuance until 2007, and redemptions until 2009.

11 For a similar viewpoint, see also *The Edge* (9 October 2013).

12 A similar scheme had been introduced by Singapore's Central Provident Fund in 1986.

13 *The Edge Financial Daily* (25 July 2016).

14 Securities Commission, 'Unit Trust Fund Summary of Statistics' (2011–2020).

15 *Fund Selector Asia* (9 May 2017).
16 *New Straits Times* (3 April 2018).
17 *The Star* (9 March 2017). UK property has also been very popular among Singaporean investors, with demand only slightly dampened by the Brexit referendum.
18 *The Edge* (7 July 2020).
19 Debates about introducing Shariah-compliant EPF accounts had been going on for decades. However, for many years EPF resisted such demands, citing the lack of a sufficient volume of Shariah-compliant investible assets as a major reason.
20 *The Malaysian Reserve* (20 February 2018).
21 See e.g. *The Star* (17 October 2018). Given the market share of GLICs, the 'free float of shares in the market' is very limited.
22 *The Economist* (15 August 2019); *Financial Times* (9 July 2020). Incidentally, Tim Leissner, who oversaw the transaction at Goldman, also is one of 20 individuals gratefully acknowledged in CMP2 for providing feedback and insight (Securities Commission 2011, 97). According to his settlement with the US Securities and Exchange Commission, Leissner also had to surrender US$43.7 million in ill-gotten gains.
23 *The Economist* (5 March 2016).
24 *The Edge Weekly* (19 July 2018); *The Edge Weekly* (21 June 2019).

6 Concluding remarks

In the two decades from the Asian crisis of the 1990s to the 1MDB scandal of the 2010s, the Malaysian financial system underwent significant change. The Asian crisis led to a series of reform efforts targeted at enhancing the resilience of the financial system. At the market level, bank consolidations were pursued, capital markets strengthened and Islamic finance became firmly entrenched in the Malaysian financial system. On the policy front, financial policymakers introduced new planning frameworks and very proactively inserted themselves into regional and international regulatory networks. However, these developments have bypassed much scholarly attention, especially at a time when 1MDB has become virtually synonymous with the worst financial scandal in Malaysia's history. If we add to this that socio-economically suboptimal financialisation has thrived in combination with significant state intervention, we arrive at a complex puzzle: how can it be that a country like Malaysia becomes significantly more financially developed, yet at the same time maintains firm political control of its economy and financial system? The answer to this puzzle is rooted in a better understanding of the relationships that underpin both progress with financial development and progressive financialisation, and the relationship between these two phenomena.

There has been growing academic and public interest in the political economy of financial policymaking in Malaysia. In particular, the various entanglements between business and politics, and between government and business have been subjected to sustained scrutiny. At the same time, there has been a strong push in studies of financialisation to move beyond analyses of the experience of mainly the US and the UK, and examine how processes of financialisation unfold in developing and emerging economies. A third strand of inquiry focuses on the emergence of Islamic finance and the question of the extent to which it challenges or reasserts the current global financial order. Bringing these different strands of scholarship together, this book has examined how intersecting dynamics of financial development and financialisation have played out in the Malaysian context of a rather distinctive form of ethnically stratified state capitalism that is a legacy of its colonial history.

In so doing, my starting claim was that to understand financial development in the Malaysian context, its progress and reversals, more attention needs to be paid to the relationships that underpin it. To this end, I have sought to scrutinise the history, practice and politics of financial development in Malaysia. This approach resonates with more profound concerns in the political economy literature, namely the changing relationship between states and markets, and the supposed retreat or reassertion of the state at a time of (financial) globalisation. The fact that Malaysia is still a developing country, albeit at the cusp of becoming a high-income country, makes its experience significant for a large range of countries in the Global South, and the lessons that can be learnt from it the more important. Along these lines, this book has also cast a light on the evolving role of the state in conjunction with broader processes of development and marketisation, as they relate specifically to finance.

Looking at Malaysia from the outside, it appears that the country has wholeheartedly subscribed to the Anglo-American model of a market-oriented financial system in which capital markets increasingly replace banks in their traditional functions. The global financial crisis of 2008–2009 has put the viability of this model, and the specific notion of financial development that it is predicated upon, into question. Moreover, like in the financialised economies of the UK and the US, in Malaysia financial development has played a role in accentuating inequalities of opportunity and wealth. Similarly, in all three countries practices of rent-seeking have been widespread, something that is particularly apparent regarding the taxation of wealth.

Nevertheless, in contrast to the UK and US, in Malaysia state control of the economy and the financial system remains firmly entrenched. Through its government-linked investment companies, the state is the single largest shareholder in the economy, including of the banking sector. Unlike in the US and UK, in Malaysia this is not a story of powerful bankers pushing back against the state. Indeed, major Malaysian banks are very much servants of their GLIC shareholders, and, for example, the pay of government-linked bank CEOs lags behind that of their more private sector counterparts, in both domestic and international comparison. Financial development has, somewhat ironically, consolidated the shift towards the shareholding state.

In this book, I have demonstrated how both financialisation and state control of the financial sector have been thriving on a combination of state interventionism and selected pro-market reforms. Much of this interventionism is justified by the ethnically stratified nature of Malaysian capitalism, but it also serves to reassert this stratification as a form of political control. Malaysia's distinctive form of shareholding state capitalism and dynamics of financialisation have been mutually reinforcing, but much of this has been coincidental rather than by design. Lingering memories of the Asian crisis among regulators and market practitioners, reinforced by the global financial crisis of 2008–2009, mean there is a certain scepticism of efficient market claims.[1]

In this sense, the shift towards shareholder-value orientation during the premiership of Abdullah Badawi was never primarily about maximising shareholder value but about clarifying the relationship between GLCs and their GLIC shareholders. Thus, for example, it did not result in the same sort of reckless financial engineering prevalent in the US and the UK that results from share prices being paramount and thus seeks to turn companies into financial assets. In so doing, shareholder-value orientation has nevertheless played a role in empowering managerial elites necessary to sustaining Malaysia's distinctive model of ethnically stratified state capitalism (cf. Knafo and Dutta 2020; see also Gomez 2017, 194–203). Together with the push in support of Islamic finance, this was clearly aimed at nurturing a Bumiputera professional class. Its professional values then sat increasingly at odds with moves during the premiership of Najib Razak to reassert greater government influence over GLICs and, indeed, establish 1MDB as a special-purpose GLIC.

Following its celebratory embrace in the late 1990s and early 2000s, in recent years, a more critical understanding of financial development has emerged (Sahay *et al.* 2015). The global financial crisis of 2008 clearly demonstrated the dangers of speculative product innovation. The opportunities it creates for excessive leverage – and lack of market scrutiny – have also played a role in the 1MDB scandal.

In Malaysia, there has been a long history of domestic institutional investors stepping in as investors-of-last resort at times of crisis, facilitated by close political-business ties. This system has significant benefits in a context where capital flows to developing and emerging economies remain volatile (Bortz and Kaltenbrunner 2018, 383). It allows the state to coordinate rather effectively its economic response in times of stress. In so doing, it reduces vulnerability to the herd behaviour of international investors and currency overshooting to which portfolio investment flows to developing countries are especially prone. However, over time it can also undermine accountability and contribute to an inefficient allocation of funds. In consequence, to understand financial development and its (more or less great) reversals it is imperative to pay attention to its political nature and avoid seeing it merely as a technical challenge. This insight also holds important lessons for the design of meaningful financial reforms, aimed at achieving broader socio-economic progress and not just intended for the betterment of small groups of well-connected elites.

Malaysia is by no means the only country that has undergone a process of far-reaching financial change and experienced concomitant financialisation. In its own way, it has sought to chart an alternative path. In this regard, its full embrace of Islamic finance stands out. Since the Asian financial crisis, Malaysian financial policymakers have not only further strengthened their efforts to consolidate the banking sector and develop the local capital market but they have done so with specific emphasis on developing Islamic financial markets. In so doing, they have played an increasingly influential role in regional and international networks, and many countries, especially in the Muslim world, are keen to emulate Malaysia's success. Islamic financial products have to be structured in a way that they comply with the prohibitions and meet requirements of Shariah. Therefore, in Islamic finance, the purpose of a financial transaction is subject to scrutiny. However, purpose has to be considered in context, especially if links between Islamic finance and financialisation are to be disentangled.

Otherwise, there is a risk that Islamic finance, despite its ambitions to provide economically and socially purposeful financing, contributes to economically and socially suboptimal financialisation dynamics. Along these lines, there has been a growing interest in and support for the development of Islamic financial products linked to housing, health care, education and retirement. Of course, these are all eminently socially purposeful things. However, they are also increasingly seen as being something that is efficiently taken care of by the market. In societal terms, this puts the onus on the individual to provide for their own shelter, health, education and old age and thus effectively desocialises many of life's risks. In the context of financialisation, nonetheless, this is not only a question of who provides these collective goods and at what price but also how finance can transform incentives. And indeed, investments in housing, health care, education and retirement plans are not only corollaries of a growing middle class, but tend to come with expectations about the growing monetisation of these sectors and appreciation of their value.

More recently, there has been growing interest in the notion of 'subordinated' financialisation as capturing financialisation dynamics in developing and emerging economies at the lower end of the international currency hierarchy. Malaysia is certainly exposed to volatility from international capital flows. Yet, at the same time, there are significant domestic pools of capital, with the value of assets currently managed by GLICs being approximately equal to Malaysian GDP. Nevertheless, given the primacy of dividends in the Malaysian political economy, it would be inaccurate to claim that GLICs are typical patient investors. As a consequence, they lack the long-term horizon necessary for investments in productive capacity building. Moreover, in the period since the Asian crisis, there have been emerging tensions between GLICs investing their funds abroad to generate yields and investing funds locally to shore up domestic markets. Thus, a period of greater outward orientation after the global financial crisis was followed by a call to repatriate funds in the wake of the 1MDB scandal. Likewise, under Pakatan Harapan GLICs were once more encouraged to seek investment opportunities overseas. In their own ways, both these strategies can contribute to performance legitimacy in terms of being able to either declare high dividends or mitigate phases of market stress. However, they also act as substantial obstacles to GLICs taking a long view. It remains to be seen what will happen now, with the global economy being so drastically affected by COVID-19.

There has been a widespread consensus on the importance of developing financial systems, specifically in so-called 'emerging' or 'frontier' economies. But there exist significant differences between financial development in theory and in practice. In this book, I have argued that a consensus in favour of financial development pre-empts fundamental debates about the role of finance in economy and society and the socioeconomic and distributive implications of specific mechanisms of creating and allocating credit. The dynamics of inclusion and exclusion that are generated by the very process of financial development have to be problematised more. It is a dangerous fallacy to consider financial exclusion as extraneous in this regard. Likewise, new vulnerabilities and inequalities that are being accentuated – if not outright caused – by financial change have to be put more under the spotlight.

To this end, we have to ask questions such as 'who benefits from financial reforms?', 'how do financial reforms affect the poorest in society?' and, particularly with regard to the notion of financial inclusion, 'inclusion in what specifically?'. An honest engagement with such questions will deliver far from straightforward answers. But they are very necessary to be asked if finance is to be harnessed for the greater good of society. Otherwise, the widely pursued ambition of financial development will be little more than a significant driver of socially suboptimal financialisation dynamics. More attention should be paid to the question of what can be done to address this.

Note

1 Until today, the crisis serves as an important reference point for Malaysian financial policymakers and market practitioners, much more so than in neighbouring Indonesia and Singapore.

Appendix A
Ownership structure of Malaysian banks

Compiled by Ana Fraga

I) Total assets and market capitalisation of selected banks

Group	Total Assets (RM Million)
Maybank Group	834,413
CIMB Group Holdings Berhad	573,246
Public Bank Berhad	432,831
RHB Bank Berhad	257,592
Hong Leong Bank Berhad	237,883#
AMMB Holdings Berhad	158,793
BIMB Holdings Berhad	77,263
Affin Bank Berhad	68,341
Alliance Bank Malaysia Berhad	56,521
Malaysia Building Society Berhad (MBSB)	50,710
Bank Muamalat Malaysia Berhad	22,886
Kenanga Investment Bank Berhad	6,631

Source: Annual Reports; financial year ending in either March 2019 or December 2019

Notes: Holding Group as applicable

data for June 2019

Group	Market Capitalisation (RM Million)
Maybank Group	97,125
Public Bank Berhad	75,469
CIMB Group Holdings Berhad	51,100
RHB Bank Berhad	23,178
Hong Leong Bank Berhad	21,300#
AMMB Holdings Berhad	13,700
BIMB Holdings Berhad	7,763
Alliance Bank Malaysia Berhad	6,332
Malaysia Building Society Berhad (MBSB)	4,263*
Affin Bank Berhad	3,773
Kenanga Investment Bank Berhad	384*

Source: Annual Reports; financial year ending in either March 2019 or December 2019

Notes: Holding Group as applicable

data for June 2019; * Bloomberg

II) List of top 15 shareholders of selected commercial banks

Affin Bank Berhad

List of top 15 shareholders as at 31 May 2020

No.	Name	Shareholdings (%)
1	LEMBAGA TABUNG ANGKATAN TENTERA	35.33
2	MAYBANK NOMINEES (ASING) SDN BHD THE BANK OF EAST ASIA LIMITED HONG KONG FOR THE BANK OF EASTASIA LIMITED (INVESTMENT AC)	23.56
3	BOUSTEAD HOLDINGS BERHAD ACCOUNT NON-TRADING	20.73
4	CITIGROUP NOMINEES (TEMPATAN) SDN BHD EMPLOYEES PROVIDENT FUND BOARD	6.82
5	AMANAHRAYA TRUSTEES BERHAD AMANAH SAHAM BUMIPUTERA	1.10
6	CITIGROUP NOMINEES (ASING) SDN BHD CBNY FOR DIMENSIONAL EMERGING MARKETS VALUE FUND	0.48
7	CITIGROUP NOMINEES (TEMPATAN) SDN BHD EXEMPT AN FOR AIA BHD	0.30
8	CITIGROUP NOMINEES (ASING) SDN BHD CBNY FOR EMERGING MARKET CORE EQUITY PORTFOLIO DFA INVESTMENT DIMENSIONS GROUP INC	0.20
9	PUBLIC NOMINEES (ASING) SDN BHD PLEDGED SECURITIES ACCOUNT FOR MAYLAND PARKVIEW SDN BHD (KLC)	0.14
10	HSBC NOMINEES (ASING) SDN BHD JPMCB, NA FOR AUSTRALIANSUPER	0.12
11	CIMB GROUP NOMINEES (AING) SDN BHD EXEMPT AN FOR DBS BANK LTD (SFS)	0.11
12	PUBLIC NOMINEES (TEMPATAN) SDN BHD PLEDGE SECURITIES ACCOUNT FOR CHEAM HENG MING (E-KTN/RAU)	0.11
13	MAYBANK SECURITIES NOMINEES (ASING) SDN BHD MAYBANK KIM ENG SECURITIES PTE LTD FOR LIM SHIANG LIANG (LIN XIANGLIANG)	0.11
14	KEY DEVELOPMENT SDN.BERHAD	0.10
15	KENANGA NOMINEES (TEMPATAN) SDN BHD PLEDGED SECURITIES ACCOUNT FOR HII YU HO	0.10

Source: Affin Bank Berhad Analysis of Shareholdings

Alliance Bank Malaysia Berhad

List of top 15 shareholders as at 31 December 2019

No.	Name	Shareholdings (%)
1	CIMB GROUP NOMINEES (TEMPATAN) SDN BHD EXEMPT AN FOR DBS BANK LTD (SFS)	29.06
2	CITIGROUP NOMINEES (TEMPATAN) SDN BHD EMPLOYEES PROVIDENT FUND BOARD	9.91
3	FOCUS ASIA STRATEGIES LTD.	4.75
4	MEDIMETRO (M) SDN BHD	3.62
5	FIELDS EQUITY MANAGEMENT LTD	2.03
6	CITIGROUP NOMINEES (TEMPATAN) SDN BHD GREAT EASTERN LIFE ASSURANCE (MALAYSIA) BERHAD (PAR 1)	1.92
7	CITIGROUP NOMINEES (TEMPATAN) SDN BHD EXEMPT AN FOR AIA BHD	1.72
8	CARTABAN NOMINEES (TEMPATAN) SDN BHD PAMB FOR PRULINK EQUITY FUND	1.44
9	EDEN ENGINEERING SDN BHD	1.27
10	HSBC NOMINEES (ASING) SDN BHD JPMCB NA FOR VANGUARD TOTAL INTERNATIONAL STOCK INDEX FUND	1.17
11	HSBC NOMINEES (ASING) SDN BHD JPMCB NA FOR VANGUARD EMERGING MARKETS STOCK INDEX FUND	1.03
12	MAYBANK NOMINEES (TEMPATAN) SDN BHD MAYBANK TRUSTEES BERHAD FOR PUBLIC REGULAR SAVINGS FUND (N14011940100)	0.97
13	CITIGROUP NOMINEES (TEMPATAN) SDN BHD KUMPULAN WANG PERSARAAN (DIPERBADANKAN) (VCAM EQUITY FD)	0.95
14	CARTABAN NOMINEES (ASING) SDN BHD BCSL CLIENT AC PB CAYMAN CLIENTS	0.90
15	CITIGROUP NOMINEES (ASING) SDN BHD CBNY FOR DIMENSIONAL EMERGING MARKETS VALUE FUND	0.87

Source: Alliance Bank Malaysia Berhad Ownership Structure

AmBank (M) Berhad (AMMB Holdings Berhad)
List of top 15 shareholders as at 31 May 2019

No.	Name	Shareholdings (%)
1	ANZ FUNDS PTY LIMITED	23.78
2	CITIGROUP NOMINEES (TEMPATAN) SDN BHD EMPLOYEES PROVIDENT FUND BOARD	6.92
3	AMCORP GROUP BERHAD	4.60
4	CIMB GROUP NOMINEES (TEMPATAN) SDN BHD CIMB BANK BERHAD (EDP 2)	3.87
5	CIMB GROUP NOMINEES (TEMPATAN) SDN BHD PLEDGED SECURITIES ACCOUNT FOR AMCORP GROUP BERHAD (AGB CBC2)	3.60
6	CIMSEC NOMINEES (TEMPATAN) SDN BHD PLEDGED SECURITIES ACCOUNT FOR AMCORP GROUP BERHAD (EDG)	3.05
7	AMANAHRAYA TRUSTEES BERHAD AMANAH SAHAM BUMIPUTERA	2.64
8	KUMPULAN WANG PERSARAAN (DIPERBADANKAN)	2.49
9	AMANAHRAYA TRUSTEES BERHAD AMANAH SAHAM MALAYSIA 2 - WAWASAN	2.36
10	HSBC NOMINEES (TEMPATAN) SDN BHD PLEDGED SECURITIES ACCOUNT FOR AMCORP GROUP BERHAD	1.47
11	AMANAHRAYA TRUSTEES BERHAD AMANAH SAHAM MALAYSIA 3	1.40
12	CARTABAN NOMINEES (ASING) SDN BHD EXEMPT AN FOR STATE STREET BANK & TRUST COMPANY (WEST CLT OD67)	1.22
13	AMANAHRAYA TRUSTEES BERHAD AMANAH SAHAM MALAYSIA	1.18
14	HSBC NOMINEES (ASING) SDN BHD JPMCB NA FOR VANGUARD EMERGING MARKETS STOCK INDEX FUND	1.08
15	CARTABAN NOMINEES (TEMPATAN) SDN BHD PAMB FOR PRULINK EQUITY FUND	1.07

Source: AMMB Holdings Berhad Analysis of Shareholdings

CIMB Bank Berhad

List of top 5 shareholders as at 30 April 2020

No.	Name	Shareholdings (%)
1	KHAZANAH NASIONAL	24.6
2	EPF (EMPLOYEES PROVIDENT FUND)	14.3
3	PNB (PERMODALAN NASIONAL BHD)	12.2
4	KWAP (KUMPULAN WANG PERSARAAN)	6.7
5	OTHERS	42.2

Source: CIMB Group Holdings Berhad Shareholding Information

Hong Leong Bank Berhad
List of top 15 shareholders as at 30 August 2019

No.	Name	Shareholdings (%)
1	HONG LEONG COMPANY (MALAYSIA) BERHAD	51.94
2	GUOCO GROUP LIMITED	25.37
3	KUMPULAN WANG PERSARAAN (DIPERBADANKAN)	1.41
4	CITIGROUP NOMINEES (TEMPATAN) SDN BHD EMPLOYEES PROVIDENT FUND BOARD	1.23
5	CITIGROUP NOMINEES (TEMPATAN) SDN BHD EMPLOYEES PROVIDENT FUND BOARD (NOMURA)	1.03
6	RHB TRUSTEES BERHAD EXEMPT AN FOR HONG LEONG FINANCIAL GROUP BERHAD (HLFG-ESS)	0.83
7	SOFT PORTFOLIO SDN. BHD.	0.58
8	TAN SRI DATO' SERI KHALID AHMAD BIN SULAIMAN	0.48
9	CITIGROUP NOMINEES (ASING) SDN BHD EXEMPT AN FOR CITIBANK NEW YORK (NORGES BANK 14)	0.48
10	TAN SRI QUEK LENG CHAN	0.47
11	CITIGROUP NOMINEES (TEMPATAN) SDN BHD EXEMPT AN FOR AIA BHD.	0.43
12	CHUA HOLDINGS SDN BHD	0.43
13	CARTABAN NOMINEES (ASING) SDN BHD EXEMPT AN FOR STATE STREET BANK & TRUST COMPANY (WEST CLT OD67)	0.41
14	HONG BEE HARDWARE COMPANY, SDN. BERHAD	0.40
15	CITIGROUP NOMINEE (ASING) SDN BHD EXEMPT AN FOR BANK OF SINGAPORE LIMITED (FOREIGN)	0.36

Source: Hong Leong Financial Group Berhad Annual Report 2019, 307–308

Malayan Banking Berhad
List of top 15 shareholders as at 31 March 2020

No.	Name	Shareholdings (%)
1	AMANAHRAYA TRUSTEES BERHAD B/O: AMANAH SAHAM BUMIPUTERA	34.68
2	CITIGROUP NOMINEES (TEMPATAN) SDN BHD B/O: EMPLOYEES PROVIDENT FUND BOARD	12.48
3	PERMODALAN NASIONAL BERHAD	7.76
4	KUMPULAN WANG PERSARAAN (DIPERBADANKAN)	4.69
5	AMANAHRAYA TRUSTEES BERHAD B B/O: AMANAH SAHAM MALAYSIA 2 - WAWASAN	2.56
6	AMANAHRAYA TRUSTEES BERHAD B B/O: AMANAH SAHAM MALAYSIA	1.70
7	AMANAHRAYA TRUSTEES BERHAD B B/O: AMANAH SAHAM MALAYSIA 3	1.05
8	HSBC NOMINEES (ASING) SDN BHD B/O: JPMCB NA FOR VANGUARD TOTAL INTERNATIONAL STOCK INDEX FUND	0.96
9	CARTABAN NOMINEES (ASING) SDN BHD B/O: EXEMPT AN FOR STATE B/O: STREET BANK & TRUST COMPANY (WEST CLT OD67)	0.91
10	AMANAHRAYA TRUSTEES BERHAD B/O: AMANAH SAHAM BUMIPUTERA 2	0.90
11	CARTABAN NOMINEES (ASING) SDN BHD B/O: GIC PRIVATE LIMITED FOR GOVERNMENT OF SINGAPORE (C)	0.86
12	CITIGROUP NOMINEES (TEMPATAN) SDN BHD B/O: GREAT EASTERN LIFE ASSURANCE (MALAYSIA) BERHAD (PAR 1)	0.80
13	HSBC NOMINEES (ASING) SDN BHD B/O: JPMCB NA FOR VANGUARD EMERGING MARKETS STOCK INDEX FUND	0.79
14	CARTABAN NOMINEES (TEMPATAN) SDN BHD B/O: PAMB FOR PRULINK EQUITY FUND	0.77
15	CITIGROUP NOMINEES (TEMPATAN) SDN BHD B/O: EXEMPT AN FOR AIA BHD.	0.75

Source: Malayan Banking Berhad Top Shareholders

Public Bank Berhad

List of top 15 shareholders as at 30 April 2020

No.	Name	Shareholdings (%)
1	CONSOLIDATED TEH HOLDINGS SDN BERHAD	21.64
2	CITIGROUP NOMINEES (TEMPATAN) SDN BHD EMPLOYEES PROVIDENT FUND BOARD	14.61
3	KUMPULAN WANG PERSARAAN (DIPERBADANKAN)	4.09
4	CARTABAN NOMINEES (ASING) SDN BHD EXEMPT AN FOR STATE STREET BANK & TRUST COMPANY (WEST CLT OD67)	1.95
5	HSBC NOMINEES (ASING) SDN BHD JPMCB NA FOR VANGUARD TOTAL INTERNATIONAL STOCK INDEX FUND	1.41
6	AMANAHRAYA TRUSTEES BERHAD AMANAH SAHAM BUMIPUTERA	1.40
7	CARTABAN NOMINEES (ASING) SDN BHD GIC PRIVATE LIMITED FOR GOVERNMENT OF SINGAPORE (C)	1.24
8	CITIGROUP NOMINEES (TEMPATAN) SDN BHD GREAT EASTERN LIFE ASSURANCE (MALAYSIA) BERHAD (PAR 1)	1.24
9	AMANAHRAYA TRUSTEES BERHAD AMANAH SAHAM MALAYSIA	1.20
10	HSBC NOMINEES (ASING) SDN BHD JPMCB NA FOR VANGUARD EMERGING MARKETS STOCK INDEX FUND	1.14
11	CARTABAN NOMINEES (TEMPATAN) SDN BHD PAMB FOR PRULINK EQUITY FUND	1.10
12	LPI CAPITAL BHD	1.10
13	UOB KAY HIAN NOMINEES (ASING) SDN BHD EXEMPT AN FOR UOB KAY HIAN PTE LTD (A/C CLIENTS)	0.79
14	AMANAHRAYA TRUSTEES BERHAD AMANAH SAHAM MALAYSIA 2 – WAWASAN	0.64
15	TAN SRI DATO' SRI DR. TEH HONG PIOW	0.64

Source: Public Bank Berhad Annual Report 2019, 244

RHB Bank Berhad

List of top 15 shareholders as at 28 February 2020

No.	Name	Shareholdings (%)
1	CITIGROUP NOMINEES (TEMPATAN) SDN BHD EMPLOYEES PROVIDENT FUND BOARD	41.72
2	OSK HOLDINGS BERHAD	4.74
3	RHB NOMINEES (ASING) SDN BHD AABAR INVESTMENTS PJS	4.23
4	AMANAHRAYA TRUSTEES BERHAD AMANAH SAHAM BUMIPUTERA	4.15
5	KUMPULAN WANG PERSARAAN (DIPERBADANKAN)	3.53
6	RHB NOMINEES (TEMPATAN) SDN BHD MALAYSIAN TRUSTEES BERHAD PLEDGED SECURITIES ACCOUNT FOR OSK HOLDINGS BHD (OSK I CM T1)	2.11
7	RHB NOMINEES (TEMPATAN) SDN BHD MALAYSIAN TRUSTEES BERHAD PLEDGED SECURITIES ACCOUNT FOR OSK HOLDINGS BHD (OSK I CM MTN T2)	1.82
8	CITIGROUP NOMINEES (TEMPATAN) SDN BHD GREAT EASTERN LIFE ASSURANCE (MALAYSIA) BERHAD (PAR 1)	1.66
9	CITIGROUP NOMINEES (TEMPATAN) SDN BHD EXEMPT AN FOR AIA BHD	1.51
10	PUBLIC INVEST NOMINEES (TEMPATAN) SDN BHD FOR OSK HOLDINGS BERHAD	1.46
11	AMANAHRAYA TRUSTEES BERHAD AMANAH SAHAM MALAYSIA 3	0.92
12	PERMODALAN NASIONAL BERHAD	0.89
13	CARTABAN NOMINEES (ASING) SDN BHD EXEMPT AN FOR STATE STREET BANK & TRUST COMPANY (WEST CLT OD67)	0.88
14	HSBC NOMINEES (ASING) SDN BHD JPMCB NA FOR VANGUARD TOTAL INTERNATIONAL STOCK INDEX FUND	0.71
15	CARTABAN NOMINEES (TEMPATAN) SDN BHD PAMB FOR PRULINK EQUITY FUND	0.65

Source: RHB Bank Berhad Annual Report 2019, 144

III) List of top 15 shareholders of selected Islamic banks
Bank Islam Malaysia Berhad
List of top 15 shareholders as at 5 May 2020

No.	Name	Shareholdings (%)
1	LEMBAGA TABUNG HAJI	52.97
2	CITIGROUP NOMINEES (TEMPATAN) SDN. BHD. EMPLOYEES PROVIDENT FUND BOARD	12.04
3	AMANAHRAYA TRUSTEES BERHAD AMANAH SAHAM BUMIPUTERA	7.98
4	PERMODALAN NASIONAL BERHAD	5.24
5	KUMPULAN WANG PERSARAAN (DIPERBADANKAN)	2.74
6	AMANAHRAYA TRUSTEES BERHAD AMANAH SAHAM BUMIPUTERA 2	1.86
7	AMANAHRAYA TRUSTEES BERHAD AMANAH SAHAM MALAYSIA 3	0.69
8	MAJLIS UGAMA ISLAM SABAH	0.65
9	MAYBANK NOMINEES (TEMPATAN) SDN. BHD. MTRUSTEE BERHAD FOR PRINCIPAL DALI EQUITY GROWTH FUND (UT-CIMB-DALI) (419455)	0.61
10	MAJLIS UGAMA ISLAM SABAH	0.58
11	DB (MALAYSIA) NOMINEE (TEMPATAN) SENDIRIAN BERHAD DEUTSCHE TRUESTEES MALAYSIA BERHAD FOR HONG LEONG VALUE FUND	0.51
12	AMIN BAITULMAL JOHOR	0.46
13	AMANAHRAYA TRUSTEES BERHAD AMANAH SAHAM MALAYSIA	0.46
14	CITIGROUP NOMINEES (TEMPATAN) SDN. BHD. EXEMPT AN FOR AIA BHD	0.43
15	CITIGROUP NOMINEES (ASING) SDN. BHD. EXEMPT AN FOR CITIBANK NEW YORK (NORGES BANK 14)	0.43

Source: BIMB Holdings Berhad Integrated Annual Report 2019, 334

Bank Muamalat Malaysia Berhad
List of shareholders

No.	Name	Shareholdings (%)
1	DRB-HICOM	70
2	KHAZANAH NASIONAL BERHAD	30

Source: Bank Muamalat Malaysia Berhad Shareholders

MBSB Bank Berhad

List of top 15 shareholders as at 29 April 2020

No.	Name	Shareholdings (%)
1	CITIGROUP NOMINEES (TEMPATAN) SDN BHD EMPLOYEES PROVIDENT FUND BOARD	64.485
2	MAYBANK SECURITIES NOMINEES (TEMPATAN) SDN BHD MALAYAN BANKING BERHAD (ECDG HEDGING)	3.724
3	CGS-CIMB NOMINEES (TEMPATAN) SDN BHD EXEMPT AN FOR CGS-CIMB SECURITIES (SINGAPORE) PTE LTD (RETAIL CLIENTS)	2.733
4	HSBC NOMINEES (ASING) SDN BHD EXEMPT AN FOR HSBC PRIVATE BANK (SUISSE) SA (CLIENT ASSETS)	1.853
5	RHB NOMINEES (ASING) SDN BHD TADHAMON CAPITAL BSC CLOSED	1.541
6	CIMB GROUP NOMINEES (ASING) SDN BHD EXEMPT AN FOR DBS BANK LTD (SFS-PB)	1.290
7	PERMODALAN NASIONAL BERHAD	0.998
8	RHB CAPITAL NOMINEES (TEMPATAN) SDN BHD PLEDGED SECURITIES ACCOUNT FOR FONG SILING (CEB)	0.611
9	KHAZANAH NASIONAL BERHAD	0.551
10	HSBC NOMINEES (ASING) SDN BHD JPMCB NA FOR VANGUARD EMERGING MARKETS STOCK INDEX FUND	0.483
11	HSBC NOMINEES (ASING) SDN BHD JPMCB NA FOR VANGUARD TOTAL INTERNATIONAL STOCK INDEX FUND	0.450
12	MAYBANK SECURITIES NOMINEES (TEMPATAN) SDN BHD PLEDGED SECURITIES ACCOUNT FOR HAWANG KIM LIAN	0.298
13	B-OK SDN BHD	0.261
14	HSBC NOMINEES (ASING) SDN BHD EXEMPT AN FOR CREDIT SUISSE (SG BR-TST-ASING)	0.248
15	AFFIN HWANG NOMINEES (TEMPATAN) SDN BHD PLEDGED SECURITIES ACCOUNT FOR CHUNG CHEE YANG	0.235

Source: Malaysia Building Society Berhad Shareholdings

III) List of top 15 shareholders of selected investment bank
Kenanga Investment Bank Berhad
List of top 15 shareholders as at 15 April 2020

No.	Name	Shareholdings (%)
1	CMS CAPITAL SDN BHD	21.95
2	TAN SRI DATO' PADUKA TENGKU NOOR ZAKIAH BINTI TENGKU ISMAIL	14.45
3	HSBC NOMINEES (ASING) SDN BHD EXEMPT AN FOR TOKAI TOKYO SECURITIES CO., LTD.	5.23
4	HSBC NOMINEES (ASING) SDN BHD EXEMPT AN FOR BANK JULIUS BAER & CO. LTD. (SINGAPORE BCH)	4.31
5	CAHYA MATA SARAWAK BERHAD	4.30
6	INFOTECH MARK SDN BHD	4.30
7	ABDUL AZIZ BIN HASHIM	4.26
8	AIZA BINTI ABDUL AZIZ	3.79
9	KENANGA NOMINEES (TEMPATAN) SDN BHD KOON POH KEONG	3.12
10	TMF TRUSTEES MALAYSIA BERHAD CHANNEL KNOWLEDGE SDN BHD	3.06
11	TMF TRUSTEES MALAYSIA BERHAD NAUNGAN EFEKTIF SDN BHD	2.09
12	INTER-PACIFIC EQUITY NOMINEES (TEMPATAN) SDN BHD INTER-PACIFIC CAPITAL SDN BHD	1.58
13	LIM KUAN GIN	1.45
14	HSBC NOMINEES (ASING) SDN BHD EXEMPT AN FOR CREDIT SUISSE	1.44
15	CIMB GROUP NOMINEES (ASING) SDN BHD EXEMPT AN FOR DBS BANK LTD	1.09

Source: Kenanga Investment Bank Berhad Annual Report 2019, 321

Appendix B
Major data sources

Bank Negara Malaysia, *Monthly Highlights and Statistics*, version 20 May, accessed at: www.bnm.gov.my/index.php?ch=en_publication& pg=en_msb&ac=282&lang=en&uc=2 [June 2020]

- Banking System: Classification of Loans by Sector – Series 1.20 and II.7
- Funds Raised in the Capital Market (by Public Sector) – Series 2.9
- Funds Raised in the Capital Market (by Private Sector) – Series 2.10
- New Issues of Corporate Bond and/or Sukuk – Series 2.11
- Labour Market Indicators for the Financial Services Sector – Series 3.5.12a
- List of Banking Institutions – Series 5.1

Bond and Sukuk Information Exchange (BIX), *BIX Search*, accessed at: www.bixmalaysia.com/Investor-Tools/BIX-Search [16 July 2020]

World Bank Data Bank, accessed at: https://databank.worldbank.org/home [June 2020]

- Global Financial Development: Bank Concentration – Malaysia, accessed at: https://databank.worldbank.org/reports.aspx?source=1250&series=GFDD.OI.01
- Market capitalization of listed domestic companies (% of GDP) – Malaysia, accessed at: https://data.worldbank.org/indicator/CM.MKT.LCAP.GD.ZS?locations=MY
- Deposit interest rate (%) – Malaysia, accessed at: https://data.worldbank.org/indicator/FR.INR.DPST?locations=MY
- GDP per capita (constant LCU) – Malaysia, accessed at: https://data.worldbank.org/indicator/NY.GDP.PCAP.KN?locations=MY

- GDP per capita (current US$) – Malaysia, accessed at: https://data. worldbank.org/indicator/NY.GDP.PCAP.CD?locations=MY
- Interest rate spread (lending rate minus deposit rate, %), accessed at: https://data.worldbank.org/indicator/FR.INR.LNDP
- Population, total – Malaysia, accessed at: https://data.worldbank. org/indicator/SP.POP.TOTL?locations=MY

References

Abdelal, Rawi and Laura Alfaro (2003) 'Capital and Control: Lessons from Malaysia', *Challenge* 46(4), pp. 36–53.

Agnes Paulus Jidwin, Jasman Tuyon and Rosalan Ali (2011) 'The Malaysian Employees Provident Fund's Members Investment Scheme: Survey of Fund Selection, Performance and Perceptions', *Asia-Pacific Management Accounting Journal* 6(1), pp. 47–79.

Allen, Franklin and Douglas Gale (2001) *Comparing Financial Systems*, Cambridge, MA: MIT Press.

Amsden, Alice (1989) *Asia's Next Giant: South Korea and Late Industrialization*, Oxford: Oxford University Press.

Ang, James B. (2008) *Financial Development and Growth in Malaysia*, London: Routledge.

Anwar Ibrahim (1995) 'Address to the Emerging Asian Bond Market Conference', Hong Kong, 27 June, accessed at: http://ikdasar.tripod.com/anwar/95-13.htm

Ariff, Mohamed (1988) 'Islamic Banking: A Southeast Asian Perspective', in: Mohamed Ariff (ed.) *Islamic Banking in Southeast Asia*, Singapore: Institute of Southeast Asian Studies, pp. 194.

Ariff, Mohamed (2017) 'Islamic Banking in Malaysia: The Changing Landscape', *Institutions and Economies* 9(2), pp. 1–13.

Ariff, Mohamed and Ahmad M. Khalid (2005) *Liberalization and Growth in Asia: 21st Century Challenges*, Cheltenham: Edward Elgar.

ASEAN Capital Markets Forum (2016) The ACMF Action Plan 2016–2020, ACMF, www.theacmf.org/ACMF/upload/acmfactionplan2016-2020.pdf

ASEAN Capital Markets Forum (2017) *ASEAN Green Bond Standards*, November, ACMF.

Asian Development Bank [ADB] and ASEAN Capital Markets Forum [ACMF] (2017) *ASEAN Corporate Governance Scorecard Country Reports and Assessments 2015*, Manila: Asian Development Bank.

Athukorala, Prema-Chandra (2001) *Crisis and Recovery in Malaysia: The Role of Capital Controls*, Cheltenham: Edward Elgar.

Azman Othman Luk, Karen Foong and Elaine Heung (2019) 'Banking Regulation in Malaysia: Overview', Thomson Reuters Practical Law, accessed at: https://uk.practicallaw.thomsonreuters.com/w-008-0538?transiti onType=Default&contextData=(sc.default)&firstPage=true&bhcp=1#co_ anchor_a261947

Bank Negara Malaysia [BNM] (1998) 'The East Asian Crisis – Causes, Policy Responses, Lessons and Issues', Working Paper No. 4.

Bank Negara Malaysia [BNM] (1999) 'Consolidation and Rationalisation of the Domestic Banking Institutions', Press Release, 2 August, accessed at: www.bnm.gov.my/index.php?ch=en_press&pg=en_press&ac=1374& lang=en

Bank Negara Malaysia [BNM] (2001) *Financial Sector Masterplan*, Kuala Lumpur: Bank Negara Malaysia.

Bank Negara Malaysia [BNM] (2009) 'Liberalisation of the Financial Sector', press release, 27 April, accessed at: www.bnm.gov.my/index.php?ch=en_ press&pg=en_press&ac=415&lang=en

Bank Negara Malaysia [BNM] (2011) *Financial Sector Blueprint*, Kuala Lumpur: Bank Negara Malaysia, www.bnm.gov.my/index.php?ch=en_ publication&pg=en_fsmp&ac=8&en

Bank Negara Malaysia [BNM] (2016) *Annual Report 2015*, Kuala Lumpur: Bank Negara Malaysia.

Bank Negara Malaysia [BNM] (2017) *Annual Report 2016*, Kuala Lumpur: Bank Negara Malaysia.

Bank Negara Malaysia [BNM] (2018) *Strategy Paper on Value-Based Intermediation*, Kuala Lumpur: Bank Negara Malaysia.

Bank Negara Malaysia [BNM] (2020a) *Annual Report 2019*, Kuala Lumpur: Bank Negara Malaysia.

Bank Negara Malaysia [BNM] (2020b) *Financial Stability Review 2019*, Kuala Lumpur: Bank Negara Malaysia.

Bank Negara Malaysia [BNM] (nodate) 'Financial Sector Development–Financial Inclusion', accessed at: www.bnm.gov.my/index.php?lang=en&ch=fsd& pg=en_fsd_market_infra&ac=95

Bank of Thailand (2006) *Thailand's Financial Sector Master Plan Handbook*, Bangkok: Bank of Thailand.

Beck, Thorsten, Aslı Demirgüç-Kunt and Ross Levine (1999) 'A New Database on Financial Development and Structure', World Bank Policy Research Working Paper 2146.

Bonizzi, Bruno (2013) 'Financialization in Developing and Emerging Countries', *International Journal of Political Economy* 42(4), pp. 83–107.

Bortz, Pablo G. and Annina Kaltenbrunner (2018) 'The International Dimension of Financialization in Developing and Emerging Economies', *Development and Change* 49(2), pp. 375–393.

Bowie, Alasdair (1991) *Crossing the Industrial Divide: State, Society and the Politics of Economic Transformation in Malaysia*, New York: Columbia University Press.

Bowie, Alasdair and Danny Unger (1997) *The Politics of Open Economies: Indonesia, Malaysia, the Philippines, and Thailand*, Cambridge: Cambridge University Press.

Broome, André and Joel Quirk (2015) 'Governing the World at a Distance: The Practice of Global Benchmarking', *Review of International Studies* 41(5), pp. 819–841.

Broome, André, Alexandra Homolar and Matthias Kranke (2018) 'Bad Science: International Organizations and the Indirect Power of Global Benchmarking', *European Journal of International Relations* 24(3), pp. 514–539.

Carmichael, Jeffrey and Michael Pomerleano (2002) *The Development and Regulation of Non-Bank Financial Institutions*, Washington, DC: The World Bank.

Case, William D. (2005) 'Malaysia: New Reforms, Old Continuities, Tense Ambiguities', *Journal of Development Studies* 41(2), pp. 284–309.

Chan Chee Khoon (2013) 'Healthcare Policy in Malaysia: Universalism, Targeting and Privatisation', in: Edmund Terence Gomez and Johan Saravanamuttu (eds.) *The New Economic Policy in Malaysia: Affirmative Action, Ethnic Inequalities and Social Justice*, Petaling Jaya: Strategic Information and Research Development Centre, pp. 151–173.

Chantrasmi, Mary and Tham Siew Yean (1982) 'Money, Banking, and Monetary Policy', in: E. K. Fisk and H. Osman Rani (eds.) *The Political Economy of Malaysia*, Kuala Lumpur: Oxford University Press, pp. 287–307.

Chin, James (2018) 'The Big Clean-Up in Malaysia', *The Interpreter*, 22 June, accessed at: www.lowyinstitute.org/the-interpreter/big-clean-malaysia

Chin Kok Fay (2005) 'Bank Restructuring in Malaysia', in: Wong Sook Ching, Jomo Kwame Sundaram and Chin Kok Fay (eds.) *Malaysian 'Bail Outs'? Capital Controls, Restructuring and Recovery*, Singapore: Singapore University Press, pp. 112–138.

Chin Kok Fay and Jomo Kwame Sundaram (2000) 'Financial Sector Rents in Malaysia', in: Mushtaq H. Khan and Jomo Kwame Sundaram (eds.) *Rents, Rent-Seeking and Economic Development*, Cambridge: Cambridge University Press, pp. 304–325.

Chwieroth, Jeffrey (2014) 'Fashions and Fads in Finance: The Political Foundations of Sovereign Wealth Fund Creation', *International Studies Quarterly* 58(4), pp. 752–763.

Čihák, Martin, Asli Demirgüç-Kunt, Erik Feyen and Ross Levine (2012) 'Benchmarking Financial Systems around the World', World Bank Policy Research Working Paper 6175.

CIMB (no date) 'Our Rich Heritage', accessed at: www.cimb.com/en/who-we-are/history/2010–2014.html

Cook, Malcolm (2008) *Banking Reform in Southeast Asia: The Region's Decisive Decade*, London: Routledge.

Crockett, Andrew *et al.* (2003) *Conflicts of Interest in the Financial Services Industry: What Shall We Do About Them?*, Geneva: International Centre for Monetary and Banking Studies.

Crouch, Harold (1996) *Government and Society in Malaysia*, Ithaca: Cornell University Press.

Dafe, Florence (2020) 'Ambiguity in International Finance and the Spread of Financial Norms: The Localization of Financial Inclusion in Kenya and Nigeria', *Review of International Political Economy* 27(3), pp. 500–524.

Datz, Giselle (2008) 'Governments as Market Players: State Innovation in the Global Economy', *Journal of International Affairs* 62(1), pp. 35–49.

Deeg, Richard and Iain Hardie (2016) 'What Is Patient Capital and Who Supplies It?', *Socio-Economic Review* 14(4), pp. 627–645.

Deloitte (2018) *Taxation and Investment in Malaysia 2018*, updated April, Deloitte.

Department of Statistics (2011) 'Population Distribution and Basic Demographic Characteristic Report 2010', updated 5 August, accessed at: www.dosm.gov.my/v1/index.php?r=column/cthemeByCat&cat=117&bul_id=MDMxdHZjWTk1SjFzTzNkRXYzcVZjdz09&menu_id=L0phe U43NWJwRWVSZklWdzQ4TlhUUT09#:~:text=The%202010%20 Population%20and%20Housing,formation%20of%20Malaysia%20in%20 1963.&text=Census%202010%20revealed%20that%20the,in%202000%20 (Chart%201)

El Gamal, Mahmoud and Amy Myers Jaffe (2012) *Oil, Dollars, Debt and Crises: The Curse of the Black Gold*, Cambridge: Cambridge University Press.

Elder, Laura (2017) 'Gendered Accounts of Expertise Within Islamic Finance and Financialization in Malaysia', in: Timothy P. Daniels (ed.) *Sharia Dynamics: Islamic Law and Sociopolitical Processes*, Basingstoke: Palgrave Macmillan, pp. 171–201.

Elias, Juanita (2020) *Gender Politics and the Pursuit of Competitiveness in Malaysia: Women on Board*, Abingdon: Routledge.

Elkins, Zach and Beth A. Simmons (2004) 'The Globalization of Liberalization: Policy Diffusion in the International Political Economy', *American Political Science Review* 98(1), pp. 171–189.

Employees Provident Fund [EPF] (2020) 'Our Past Dividend Rates', last updated: 24 February, accessed at: www.kwsp.gov.my/dividend

Epstein, Gerald A. (2005) 'Introduction: Financialization and the World Economy', in: Gerald A. Epstein (ed.) *Financialization and the World Economy*, London: Edward Elgar Publishing, pp. 3–16.

Epstein, Gerald A. (2019) *The Political Economy of Central Banking: Contested Control and the Power of Finance, Selected Essays of Gerald Epstein*, Cheltenham: Edward Elgar.

Ertürk, Ismail and Stefano Solari (2007) 'Banks as Continuous Reinvention', *New Political Economy* 12(3), pp. 369–388.

Evans, Peter (1995) *Embedded Autonomy: States and Industrial Transformation*, Princeton: Princeton University Press.

Faaland, Just, J. R. Parkinson and Rais Saniman (1990) *Growth and Ethnic Inequality: Malaysia's New Economic Policy*, London and New York: St. Martin's Press.

Faulconbridge, James (2019) 'Business Services and the Financing of Global Production Networks: The Case of Global Law Firms in Southeast Asia', *Journal of Economic Geography* 19(4), pp. 897–919.

Federation of Investment Managers Malaysia [FIMM] (2020) 'EPF-MIS Approved Fund List – 1 April 2020', accessed at: www.fimm.com.my/industry/analytics-statistics/epf-approved-funds/

FTSE Russell (2020) 'FTSE Bursa Malaysia KLCI – Fact Sheet: 29 May 2020', accessed at: https://research.ftserussell.com/Analytics/FactSheets/Home/DownloadSingleIssue?openfile=open&issueName=FBMKLCI&isManual=False&_ga=2.168780580.406252490.1593292762-1693371007.1593292762

Gentner, Dedre (2005) 'The Development of Relational Category Knowledge', in: Lisa Gershkoff-Stowe and David H. Rakison (eds.) *Building Object Categories in Developmental Time*, Hillsdale: Erlbaum, pp. 245–275.

Ghazali, Nazlan and Punitha Kandiah (2014) 'Financial Services Act 2013: A Significant Development in the Financial Services Industry in Malaysia', *International In-house Counsel Journal* 27(7), 1–9.

Gill, Ranjit (1985) *The Making of Malaysia Inc.: A Twenty-Five Year Review of the Securities Industry of Malaysia & Singapore*, Bruce Gale (ed.), Singapore: Pelanduk Publications.

Goldsmith, Raymond W. (1959) *The Comparative Study of Economic Growth and Structure*, New York: NBER.

Gomez, Edmund Terence (1999) *Chinese Business in Malaysia*, London: Curzon.

Gomez, Edmund Terence (2013) 'The Politics and Policies of Corporate Development: Race, Rents and Redistribution in Malaysia', in: Hal Hill, Tham Siew Yean and Ragayah Haji Mat Zin (eds.) *Malaysia's Development Challenges: Graduating from the Middle*, Abingdon: Routledge.

Gomez, Edmund Terence (2017) *Ministry of Finance Incorporated: Ownership and Control of Corporate Malaysia*, with Thirshalar Padmanabhan, Norfaryanti Kamaruddin, Sunil Bhalla and Fikri Fisal, Petaling Jaya: Strategic Information and Research Development Centre/Palgrave Macmillan.

Gomez, Edmund Terence and Jomo Kwame Sundaram (1999) *Malaysia's Political Economy: Politics, Patronage and Profits*, 2nd ed., Cambridge: Cambridge University Press.

Gomez, Edmund Terence and Elsa Lafaye De Micheaux (2017) 'Diversity of Southeast Asian Capitalisms: Evolving State-Business Relations in Malaysia', *Journal of Contemporary Asia* 47(5), pp. 792–814.

Government of Malaysia (1971) *Second Malaysia Plan, 1971–1975*, Kuala Lumpur: Government Press.

Government of Malaysia (1976) *Third Malaysia Plan, 1976–1980*, Kuala Lumpur: Government Press.

Government of Malaysia (1981) *Fourth Malaysia Plan, 1981–1985*, Kuala Lumpur: Government Press.

Government of Malaysia (1986) *Fifth Malaysia Plan, 1986–1990*, Kuala Lumpur: Government Press.

Government of Malaysia (1991) *Sixth Malaysia Plan, 1991–1996*, Kuala Lumpur: Government Press.

Government of Malaysia (1996) *Seventh Malaysia Plan, 1996–2000*, Kuala Lumpur: Government Press.

Government of Malaysia (1999) *White Paper: Status of the Malaysian Economy*, Economic Planning Unit, Kuala Lumpur: Percetakan Nasional Malaysia Berhad.

Gunasegaram, P. and KiniBiz (2018) *1MDB The Scandal That Brought Down a Government*, Petaling Jaya: SIRD.

Haggard, Stephan (2000) *The Political Economy of the Asian Financial Crisis*, Washington, DC: Institute for International Economics.

Haggard, Stephan and Chung Lee (1993) 'The Political Dimension of Finance in Economic Development', in: Stephan, Haggard, Chung Lee and Sylvia Maxfield (eds.) *The Politics of Finance in Developing Countries*, Ithaca: Cornell University Press, pp. 3–20.

Hamilton-Hart, Natasha (2002) *Asian States, Asian Bankers: Central Banking in Southeast Asia*, Ithaca and London: Cornell University Press.

Hamilton-Hart, Natasha (2016) '1MDB Scandal Reveals Tangled Web of Global Finance', *East Asia Forum*, 30 August, accessed at: www.eastasiaforum.org/2016/08/30/1mdb-scandal-reveals-tangled-web-of-global-finance/

Hirschman, Albert O. (1958) *The Strategy of Economic Development*, New Haven: Yale University Press.

Horii, K. (1991) 'Disintegration of the Colonial Economic Legacies and Social Restructuring in Malaysia', *The Developing Economies* 29(4), pp. 281–313.

IOSCO (2004) *Islamic Capital Market Fact Finding Report*, Report of the Islamic Capital Market Task Force of the International Organization of Securities Commissions, Madrid: IOSCO.

Islam, Iyanatul and Anis Chowdhury (2000) *The Political Economy of East Asia: Post-Crisis Debates*, Oxford: Oxford University Press.

Ismail Muhd Salleh (1982) 'Public Finance', in: E. K. Fisk and H. Osman Rani (eds.) *The Political Economy of Malaysia*, Kuala Lumpur: Oxford University Press, pp. 308–340.

Jesudason, James V. (1989) *Ethnicity and the Economy: The State, Chinese Business and Multinationals in Malaysia*, Singapore: Oxford University Press.

Johnson, Simon and James Kwak (2010) *13 Bankers: The Wall Street Takeover and the Next Financial Meltdown*, New York: Pantheon Books.

Jomo Kwame Sundaram (1990) *Growth and Structural Change in the Malaysian Economy*, Basingstoke and London: Macmillan.

Jomo Kwame Sundaram and E. Terence Gomez (2000) 'The Malaysian Development Dilemma', in: Mushtaq H. Khan and Jomo Kwame Sundaram (eds.) *Rents, Rent-Seeking and Economic Development*, Cambridge: Cambridge University Press, pp. 274–303.

Jomo Kwame Sundaram and Tan Wooi Syn (2005) 'Privatization and Re-Nationalization in Malaysia: A Survey', Unpublished Working Paper, accessed at: www.jomoks.org/research/pdf/IPD_Privatization_Renationalization.pdf

Jones, Emily and Alexandra O. Zeitz (2019) 'Regulatory Convergence in the Financial Periphery: How Interdependence Shapes Regulators' Decisions', *International Studies Quarterly* 63(4), pp. 908–922.

Karwowski, Ewa and Engelbert Stockhammer (2017) 'Financialisation in Emerging Economies: A Systematic Overview and Comparison with Anglo-Saxon Economies', *Economic and Political Studies* 5(1), pp. 60–86.

Kemplay, Marie (2020) 'Top 1000 World Banks 2020', *The Banker*, 1 July, accessed at: www.thebanker.com/Top-1000-World-Banks/Top-1000-World-Banks-2020

Khan, Ashraf (2018) 'Legal Protection: Liability and Immunity Arrangements of Central Banks and Financial Supervisors', IMF Working Paper WP/18/176.

Khoo Boo Teik (1995) *Paradoxes of Mahathirism: An Intellectual Biography of Mahathir Mohamad*, Kuala Lumpur and Oxford: Oxford University Press.

Khoo Boo Teik (2003) *Beyond Mahathir: Malaysian Politics and Its Discontents*, London: Zed.

Khoo Boo Teik (2018) 'Political Turbulence and Stalemate in Contemporary Malaysia: Oligarchic Reconstitutions and Insecurities', *TRaNS: Trans-Regional and –National Studies of Southeast Asia* 6(2), pp. 227–251.

Khor, Martin Kok Peng (1983) *The Malaysian Economy*, Kuala Lumpur: Marican and Sons.

Knafo, Samuel and Jahil S. Dutta (2020) 'The Myth of the Shareholder Revolution and the Financialization of the Firm', *Review of International Political Economy* 27(3), pp. 476–499.

KPMG (2019) 'Corporate Tax: A Critical Part of ESG', *KPMG Insights*, accessed at: https://home.kpmg/xx/en/home/insights/2019/03/corporate-tax-a-critical-part-of-esg.html

Lai, Jikon (2012) 'Khazanah Nasional: Malaysia's Treasure Trove', *Journal of the Asia Pacific Economy* 17(2), pp. 236–252.

Lai, Jikon, Lena Rethel and Kerstin Steiner (2017) 'Conceptualizing Dynamic Challenges to Global Financial Diffusion: Islamic Finance and the Grafting of Sukuk', *Review of International Political Economy* 24(6), pp. 958–979.

Langley, Paul (2020) 'Assets and Assetization in Financialized Capitalism', *Review of International Political Economy*, forthcoming.

Lau Zheng Zhou and Nur Zulaikha Azmi (2020) 'GLIC Footprint in the Private Sector: Policy Dilemma', *Brief Ideas* No. 21, Institute for Democracy and Economic Affairs, April.

Lee, Hwok-Aun and Muhammed Abdul Khalid (2020) 'Is Inequality Really Declining in Malaysia?', *Journal of Contemporary Asia* 50(1), pp. 14–35.

Lee, S. Y. and Y. C. Jao (1982) *Financial Structures and Monetary Policy in Southeast Asia*, London: Macmillan.

Lembaga Tabung Angkatan Tentera (no date) 'Statistik Dividen', accessed at: www.ltat.org.my/borg/arkib/Statistikdividen2014e.pdf

Lembaga Tabung Haji (no date) 'Data & Statistik (5) Tahun', accessed at: www.tabunghaji.gov.my/ms/korporat/informasi-korporat/data-statistik-5-tahun

Levine, Ross (1997) 'Financial Development and Economic Growth: Views and Agenda', *Journal of Economic Literature* 35(2), pp. 688–726.

Lim Mah Hui (1981) *Ownership and Control of the One Hundred Largest Corporations in Malaysia*, Kuala Lumpur: Oxford University.

Lin, Justin Yifu, Xifang Sun and Ye Jiang (2009) 'Toward a Theory of Optimal Financial Structure', Policy Research Working Paper 5038, The World Bank

Madrid, Raúl L. (1992) *Overexposed: US Banks Confront the Third World Debt Crisis*, Boulder: Westview Press.

Mahathir Mohamad (1991) 'Vision 2020 [Wawasan 2020]', speech presented at the Malaysian Business Council, Kuala Lumpur, February 28; published for the Malaysian Business Council by the Institute of Strategic and International Studies (ISIS) Malaysia, Kuala Lumpur: Setiakawan Printers Sdn Bhd.

Marcussen, Marcus (2007) 'Central Banks on the Move', *Journal of European Public Policy* 12(5), pp. 903–923.

Martin, Randy (2002) *Financialization of Daily Life*, Philadelphia: Temple University Press.

Maurer, Bill (2005) *Mutual Life, Limited: Islamic Banking, Alternative Currencies, Lateral Reason*, Princeton: Princeton University Press.

Mawdudi, Sayyid Abul A'lā (2011) *First Principles of Islamic Economics*, Khurshid Ahmad (ed.); translated by Ahmad Imam Sharaq Hashemi, Markfield: Islamic Foundation.

Milne, Robert S. (1986) 'Malaysia – Beyond the New Economic Policy', *Asian Survey* 26(12), pp. 1364–1382.

Moschella, M. and E. Tsingou (2013) (eds.) *Great Expectations, Slow Transformation: Incremental Change in Post-Crisis Regulation*, Colchester: ECPR Press.

Mosley, Layna (2000) 'Room to Move: International Financial Markets and National Welfare States', *International Organization* 54(4), pp. 737–773.

Mosley, Layna (2003) *Global Capital, National Governments*, Cambridge: Cambridge University Press.

Muhammed Abdul Khalid (2014) *The Colour of Inequality: Ethnicity, Class, Income and Wealth in Malaysia*, Petaling Jaya: MPH Publishing.

MyPF (no date) 'ASB Historical Returns from 1990 to 2019', accessed at: https://mypf.my/2019/12/18/asb-historical-returns-1990-to-2019/

Nelson, Joan M. (ed.) (1990) *Economic Crisis and Policy Choice: The Politics of Adjustment in Less Developed Countries*, Princeton: Princeton University Press.

Nelson, Joan M., Jacob Meerman and Abdul Rahman Embong (eds.) (2008) *Globalization and National Autonomy: The Experience of Malaysia*, Singapore: ISEAS.

Nesadurai, Helen E. S. (2000) 'In Defence of National Economic Autonomy? Malaysia's Response to the Financial Crisis', *The Pacific Review* 13(1), pp. 73–113.

Nesadurai, Helen E. S. (2011) 'Economic Surveillance as a New Mode of Regional Governance: Contested Knowledge and the Politics of Risk

Management in East Asia', *Australian Journal of International Affairs* 63(3), pp. 361–375.

Nesadurai, Helen E. S. (2018) 'New Constellations of Social Power: States and Transnational Private Governance of Palm Oil Sustainability in Southeast Asia', *Journal of Contemporary Asia* 48(2), pp. 204–229.

Nölke, Andreas, Tobias ten Brink, Simone Claar and Christian May (2015) 'Domestic Structures, Foreign Economic Policies and Global Economic Order: Implications from the Rise of Large Emerging Economies', *European Journal of International Relations* 21(3), pp. 538–567.

Nor Shamsiah Mohd Yunus (2018) 'Value Based Intermediation – Beyond Profit', Keynote Governor of the Central Bank of Malaysia, at the Global Islamic Finance Forum 2018 (GIFF), Kuala Lumpur, 3 October.

Öniş, Ziya (1991) 'The Logic of the Developmental State', *Comparative Politics* 24(1), pp. 109–126.

Otoritas Jasa Keuangan [OJK/Indonesian Financial Services Authority] (2016) *Indonesian Financial Services Sector Masterplan 2015–2019*, Jakarta: OJK, www.ojk.go.id/en/berita-dan-kegiatan/publikasi/Documents/Pages/Indonesian-Financial-Services-Sector-Master-Plan-2015–2019/MPSJKI%20OJK%20Final_Eng.pdf

Paul, Deborah L. and T. Eiko Stange (2020) 'Tax and ESG', Harvard Law School Corporate Governance Forum, 22 February, accessed at: https://corpgov.law.harvard.edu/2020/02/22/tax-and-esg/

Pepinsky, Thomas (2008) 'Institutions, Economic Recovery, and Macroeconomic Vulnerability in Indonesia and Malaysia', in: Andrew MacIntyre, T. J. Pempel and John Ravenhill (eds.) *Crisis as Catalyst: Asia's Dynamic Political Economy*, Ithaca and London: Cornell University Press, pp. 231–250.

Pepinsky, Thomas (2012) 'The Political Economy of Financial Development in Southeast Asia', in Andrew Walter and Xiaoke Zhang (eds.) *East Asian Capitalism: Diversity, Continuity, and Change*, Oxford: Oxford University Press.

Permodalan Nasional Berhad [PNB] (2020) *Annual Report 2019*, Kuala Lumpur: Permodalan Nasional Berhad.

Petry, Johannes, Jan Fichtner and Eelke Heemskerk (2019) 'Steering Capital: The Growing Private Authority of Index Providers in the Age of Passive Asset Management', *Review of International Political Economy*, online first.

Pike, Andy and Jane Pollard (2010) 'Economic Geographies of Financialization', *Economic Geography* 86(1), pp. 29–51.

Pitluck, Aaron Z. (2013) 'Islamic Banking and Finance: Alternative or Façade?', in: Karin Knorr Cetina and Alex Preda (eds.) *The Oxford Handbook of the Sociology of Finance*, Oxford: Oxford University Press.

Puthucheary, James J. (1960) *Ownership and Control in the Malayan Economy*, Singapore: Donald Moore for Eastern Universities Press.

Putrajaya Committee (2006) GLC Transformation Manual, accessed at: www.pcg.gov.my/trans_manual.asp

Rajan, Raghuram G. (2005) 'Has Financial Development Made the World Riskier?', NBER Working Paper No. 11728, November.

Rajan, Raghuram G. (2011) *Fault Lines: How Hidden Fractures Still Threaten the World Economy*, Princeton: Princeton University Press.

Rajan, Raghuram G. and Luigi Zingales (2003) 'The Great Reversals: The Politics of Financial Development in the Twentieth Century', *Journal of Financial Economics* 69(1), pp. 5–50.

Ramirez, Carlos D. and Tan Ling Hui (2003) 'Singapore Inc. Versus the Private Sector: Are Government-Linked Companies Different?', IMF Working Paper WP/03/156.

Rethel, Lena (2010a) 'The New Financial Development Paradigm and Asian Bond Markets', *New Political Economy* 15(4), pp. 493–517.

Rethel, Lena (2010b) 'Financialisation and the Malaysian Political Economy', *Globalizations* 7(4), pp. 489–506.

Rethel, Lena (2014) 'Regionalising Financial Development in East Asia', in: Yong-soo Eun and Toni Haastrup (eds.) *Regionalising Global Crises: The Financial Crisis and New Frontiers in Regional Governance*, Basingstoke: Palgrave.

Rethel, Lena (2016) 'Global Ambitions, Local Realities: The Everyday Political Economy of Islamic Finance in Malaysia', in: Juanita Elias and Lena Rethel (eds.) *The Everyday Political Economy of Southeast Asia*, Cambridge: Cambridge University Press.

Rethel, Lena (2018) 'Capital Market Development in Southeast Asia: From Speculative Crisis to Spectacles of Financialization', *Economic Anthropology* 5(2), pp. 185–197.

Rethel, Lena (2020) 'Governed Interdependence, Communities of Practice and the Production of Capital Market Knowledge in Southeast Asia', *New Political Economy* 25(3), pp. 354–369.

Rethel, Lena and Timothy J. Sinclair (2012) *The Problem with Banks*, London: Zed Books.

Rethel, Lena and Timothy J. Sinclair (2014) 'Innovation and the Entrepreneurial State in Asia: Mechanisms of Bond Market Development', *Asian Studies Review* 38(4), pp. 564–581.

Rethel, Lena, Juanita Elias and Lisa Tilley (2019) 'Tales from Two Cities: Financialisation, Consumerism and Affordable Housing in Kuala Lumpur and Jakarta', in: Johan Fischer and Jeremy Jammes (eds.) *Muslim Piety as Economy: Markets, Meaning and Morality in Southeast Asia*, Abingdon: Routledge.

Rewcastle Brown, Clare (2018) *The Sarawak Report: The Inside Story of the 1MDB Expose*, Petaling Jaya: Gerakbudaya Enterprise.

Rudnyckyj, Daromir (2019) *Beyond Debt: Islamic Experiments in Global Finance*, Chicago: University of Chicago Press.

Sahay, Ratna, Martin Čihák, Papa N'Diaye, Adolfo Barajas, Ran Bi, Diana Ayala, Yuan Gao, Annette Kyobe, Lam Nguyen, Christian Saborowski, Katsiaryna Svirydzenka and Seyed Reza Yousefi (2015) 'Rethinking Financial Deepening: Stability and Growth in Emerging Markets', IMF Staff Discussion Note SDN/15/08, May.

Salleh Harun (2002) 'The Development of Debt Markets in Malaysia', *BIS Papers* No. 11, pp. 147–150, available at: www.bis.org/publ/bppdf/bispap11m.pdf.

Searle, Peter (1999) *The Riddle of Malaysian Capitalism: Rent-Seekers or Real Capitalists?*, St. Leonards and Honolulu: Asian Studies Association of Australia.

Securities Commission [SC] (various years) *Annual Report*, Kuala Lumpur: Securities Commission.

Securities Commission [SC] (2001) *Capital Market Masterplan*, Kuala Lumpur: Securities Commission.

Securities Commission [SC] (2004) *Capital Market Development in Malaysia: History and Perspectives*, Kuala Lumpur: Securities Commission.

Securities Commission [SC] (2011) *Capital Market Masterplan 2*, Kuala Lumpur: Securities Commission.

Securities Commission [SC] (2014) *Capital Market Development in Malaysia: Growth, Competitiveness and Resilience*, Kuala Lumpur: Securities Commission.

Securities Commission [SC] (2019) *Sustainable and Responsible Investment Roadmap for the Malaysian Capital Market*, Kuala Lumpur: Securities Commission.

Securities Commission [SC] (2020) 'Private Retirement Scheme Statistics – as at 21 May 2020', accessed at: www.sc.com.my/analytics/fund-management-products

Securities Commission [SC] (no date) 'Special Incentives', accessed at: www.sc.com.my/development/islamic-capital-market/special-incentives

Sinclair, Timothy J. (2005) *The New Masters of Capital: American Bond Rating Agencies and the Politics of Creditworthiness*, Ithaca: Cornell University Press.

Singh, Supriya (1984) *Bank Negara Malaysia: The First Twenty Five Years*, Kuala Lumpur: Bank Negara Malaysia.

Skully, Michael T. and George J. Viksnins (1987) *Financing Asia's Success: Comparative Financial Development in Eight Asian Countries*, Basingstoke and London: Macmillan Press.

Strange, Susan (1986) *Casino Capitalism*, Oxford: Basil Blackwell.

Subramaniam, Vimal Prakash Rao, Rossazana Ab-Rahim and Sonia Kumari Selvarajan (2019) 'Financial Development, Efficiency, and Competition of ASEAN Banking Market', *Asia-Pacific Social Science Review* 19(3), pp. 185–202.

Syahirah Abdul Rahman, Ismail Ertürk and Julie Froud (2020) 'Financial Citizenship and Nation-Building in Malaysia: Elites' and Citizens' Perspectives', *Journal of Economic Geography* 20, pp. 225–248.

Tan, Amy Ai Fen and Stella Lee Siew Tsin (2013) 'Malaysia's New Financial Services Regulatory Framework', *Financier Worldwide*, July, accessed at: www.financierworldwide.com/malaysias-new-financial-services-regulatory-framework#.Xuprn0W2nDc

Tan Tat Wai (2003) 'The Impact of the 1997 Financial Crisis on Malaysia's Corporate Sector and Its Response', in: Colin Barlow and Francis Loh

Kok Wah (eds.) *Malaysian Economics and Politics in the New Century*, Cheltenham and Northampton: Edward Elgar, pp. 29–45.

Timewell, Stephen (2010) 'New World Order', The Banker, 6 July, www. thebanker.com/Banker-Data/Banker-Rankings/New-World-Order

Tomaskovic-Devey, Donald, Ken-Hou Lin and Nathan Meyers (2015) 'Did Financialization Reduce Economic Growth?', *Socio-Economic Review* 13(3), pp. 525–548.

UKIFC and ISRA (2020) 'Islamic Finance and the SDGs: Framing the Opportunity', Thought Leadership Series Part 1, May, accessed at: www. ukifc.com/sdg/thought-paper-1/

UN Global Compact (no date) 'Creating Markets That Deliver Greater Value to Society – Financial Markets', accessed at: www.unglobalcompact.org/ what-is-gc/our-work/financial

Verdier, Daniel (2002) *Moving Money: Banking and Finance in the Industrialized World*, New York: Cambridge University Press.

Wade, Robert (2004) *Governing the Market: Economic Theory and the Role of Government in East Asian Industrialization*, 2nd ed., Princeton: Princeton University Press.

Wade, Robert and Frank Veneroso (1998) 'The Asian Crisis: The High-Debt Model Versus the Wall Street-Treasury-IMF Complex', *New Left Review* I/ 228, pp. 3–23.

Wang, Yingyao (2015) 'The Rise of the "Shareholding State": Financialization of Economic Management in China', *Socio-Economic Review* 13(3), pp. 603–625.

Warde, Ibrahim A. (2000) *Islamic Finance in the Global Economy*, Edinburgh: Edinburgh University Press.

Weiss, Linda (1998) *The Myth of the Powerless State*, Cambridge: Cambridge University Press.

Welsh, Bridget and James Chin (eds.) (2013) *Awakening: The Abdullah Badawi Years in Malaysia*, Petaling Jaya: SIRD.

Wong Tai Chee (1990) 'Industrial Development, the New Economic Policy in Malaysia, and the International Division of Labour', *ASEAN Economic Bulletin* 7(1), pp. 106–119.

Wong Hwa Kiong and Jomo Kwame Sundaram (2005) 'Before the Storm: The Impact of Foreign Capital Inflows on the Malaysian Economy, 1966–1996', *Journal of the Asia Pacific Economy* 10(1), pp. 56–69.

Wong Sook Ching, Jomo Kwame Sundaram and Chin Kok Fay (2005) *Malaysian 'Bail Outs'? Capital Controls, Restructuring and Recovery*, Singapore: NUS Press.

World Bank (1995) *The Emerging Asian Bond Market*, Washington, DC: The World Bank.

World Economic Forum (2012) *The Financial Development Report 2012*, Geneva and New York: World Economic Forum.

Young, Kevin L. (2012) 'Transnational Regulatory Capture? An Empirical Examination of the Transnational Lobbying of the Basel Committee on

Banking Supervision', *Review of International Political Economy* 19(4), pp. 663–688.

Zainal Aznam Yusof, Awang Adek Hussin, Ismail Alowi, Lim Chee Sing and Sukhdave Singh (1996) 'Financial Reform in Malaysia', in: Gerard Caprio, Izak Atiyas and James A.Hanson (eds.) *Financial Reform: Theory and Experience*, Cambridge: Cambridge University Press, pp. 276–320.

Zeti Akhtar Aziz (2009) 'Islamic Finance and Financial Stability', Opening remarks, Governor of the Central Bank of Malaysia, at the BNM High Level Conference on Financial Stability, Bank Negara Malaysia, Kuala Lumpur, 24 November.

Zeti Akhtar Aziz (2012a) 'Internationalisation of Islamic Finance – Bridging Economies', Welcoming address by Dr Zeti Akhtar Aziz, Governor of the Central Bank of Malaysia, at the Global Islamic Finance Forum 2012, Kuala Lumpur, 19 September.

Zeti Akhtar Aziz (2012b) 'Global Financial Stability and the Internationalisation of Financial Systems in Emerging Economies', Euromoney Qatar Conference, Doha, 11 December.

Index

Abdul Aziz 42
Abdullah Badawi 35–6, 39, 87
Ahmad Mohd Don 42
Ali Abul Hassan 42
Amanah Saham Berhad (ASB) 73–4
Anwar Ibrahim 32, 35, 39
appointments systems 15
Ariff, Mohamed 63
Asian financial crisis (1997–1998)
    1–4, 13, 35–9, 47, 50, 67, 69, 85–8
assetisation 62
Association of Southeast Asian
    Nations (ASEAN): Capital
    Markets Forum 70; Collective
    Investment Scheme (CIS) 76;
    Corporate Governance Scorecard
    10; Green Bond Standards 78
Azman Othman Luk 52

bank functions 86
Bank Negara Malaysia 3–4, 20,
    26, 33–4, 41–6, 51–7, 60–5, 81;
    governors of 42
banking institutions, number and
    type of 51–2, 65
banking system 6, 17, 21–2, 51–4, 68
Barisan Nasional coalition 1,
    30–1, 36, 38
'big bang' reforms 23
bond market 10, 13, 23–5, 34,
    68–72, 82
bonds, intrinsic features of 70
Bortz, Pablo G. 19
Bretton Woods system 21
Bumiputeras 48, 73–4, 87
buzzwords, use of 20–1

capital flows 19–20, 35, 67, 87, 89
Capital Issues Committee (CIC)
    44
capital markets 6–7, 13, 24, 29, 34,
    46–8, 65, 68–77, 82, 86; widening
    and deepening of 68–70
capitalist economies 30
central bank independence 14
central bank of Malaysia see Bank
    Negara Malaysia
Chan Chee Khoon 62
chief executive officers (CEOs), pay
    of 81–2, 86
Chwieroth, Jeffrey 13
CIMB (bank) 59, 72
concentration of credit
    intermediation 22
consolidation in the banking
    sector 51–4
consumer finance 57–9, 65
Cook, Malcolm 51
corporate bonds 71–2, 82
corporate governance 69
COVID-19 pandemic 22, 37, 57,
    61
credit rating agencies 16
crony capitalism 34, 38
currency overshooting 87

Dafe, Florence 9
Daim Zainuddin 42
developing countries 6, 17, 86
disintermediation, financial 23–5
dividend payments 56, 59
domestic systematically important
    banks (D-SIBs) 53, 63

122 *Index*